Teaching Tools

for

the 21st Century

Revised Expanded Edition

By
Carolyn Coil

Pieces of Learning

CLC0378
ISBN 1-931334-72-2
© 2005 Third Revised Expanded Edition Carolyn Coil
Second Edition © 2000 Carolyn Coil
First Edition © 1997 Carolyn Coil
Cover Design by John Steele

Table of Contents

Introduction

DEDICATION

With special love to:

My parents, William and Charlotte Hendrix, who have always supported me and cheered me on in anything I have attempted to do.

Mary C. (Kitty) Walker, the very special teacher who inspired, motivated, loved, and encouraged me throughout my junior high years and who continues to be an important person in my life.

My children and grandchildren, nieces and nephews, who will live throughout the 21st century.

My husband, Doug, for his continual love and support.

ACKNOWLEDGMENTS

Special thanks to all the educators who have used the ideas presented in this book and have given me feedback about what worked best and how to make some of my "tools" function better.

Thanks to Mona Livermont for researching topics and web sites in this book.

Thank you to John Matin, DeKalb County, Georgia, who gave me suggestions for the Technology Chapter.

Thanks to Carol Dominquez, a 5th grade student at Jackson School in Seymour, Indiana, for her poem in the Cultural & Linguistic Diversity chapter.

Thanks to the Pieces of Learning staff, especially Stan and Kathy Balsamo, for their hard work, suggestions, assistance, and encouragement.

How to Use This Book

As I travel around the country presenting staff development workshops, I encounter several educational theories, ideas, and buzz words. **Learning styles, multiple intelligences, cultural diversity, inclusion, globalization, student-directed learning, new technologies,** *No Child Left Behind*, **standardized testing, adequate yearly progress,** and **alternative assessment** are some of the terms I hear. As I researched these terms, ideas, and concepts, I realized how powerful they are and the potential they hold to change the whole face of education. At the same time I realize that most teachers feel overwhelmed with the number of theories and changes they need to absorb. I know they need Tools to help them and make their enormous task easier.

A **tool** can be defined as **any instrument or device used to make the work of one's profession or occupation easier, more effective, or more efficient.** Teachers have always used a variety of Tools, from the slate and chalkboard to the personal computer. Teaching Tools also include plan books, curriculum designs, and visual organizers.

With these in mind, I feel that creating additional Tools to help teachers incorporate the new educational theories and ideas into their classrooms is important. These Tools will help teachers facilitate the learning of their students in the 21st century.

Many Teaching Tools are presented in this book. As you read, I'll introduce you to these Tools and will show examples of how to use each. You will find flexible strategies and techniques for incorporating learning styles and modalities, multiple intelligences, and Bloom's Taxonomy. You will find Tools to help you understand and manage cultural diversity, conflict, collaboration with parents, and the inclusion of special needs and gifted students. There is a chapter about assessment and one about technology. Each contains practical information to help teachers **now!**

Tools for Reflective Learning

Because of the amount and variety of information presented in this book, it is best to read the **Questions to Consider** Box you will find at the beginning of each chapter. These questions target the ideas that I discuss in the chapter. After you read a chapter, the **Reflections** Box will help you review the main concepts presented.

I have included two other Tools – reproducible pages you can use with students, parents, or other teachers and specific **Teacher Reflection Pages** – throughout the book. These **Teacher Reflection Pages** are content specific. For each topic discussed in the book, they offer questions for reflection and discussion. Use these pages individually or as part of a teacher self-assessment portfolio. However, their best use may be in a small group setting.

You are granted permission to reproduce the **Student Activities** and **Teacher Reflection** and **Teacher Information Pages** for you and your classroom only. These pages are indicated by the pencil ✏. The CD includes both PDF printable files of those pages and other customizable WORD files.

Introduction

The **Teacher Reflection** pages can guide reflective thinking about a particular topic in various group settings:

- ❑ University classes
- ❑ Site-based management teams
- ❑ Collaborative groups and teams
- ❑ Grade level or subject area planning meetings
- ❑ Faculty meetings
- ❑ Coaching/collegial support teams
- ❑ Beginning teacher programs
- ❑ Professional development sessions

Another Tool to use in reflective thinking is the **Coil 4-I Planning Model**™. Use the reproducible form of the model on page 7. This is a generic planning model that you can use individually or in any group planning session. I often use it in my staff development workshops to help participants structure their thinking and planning in implementing workshop ideas.

Use the **Coil 4-I Planning Model**™ when you are introduced to new concepts, thoughts, or theories. When you listen to a speaker, when you are in conversation with a colleague, when you are part of a decision-making team, or when you are reading or studying on your own, this Tool will help you understand what is being taught or discussed. It gives you a way to apply new concepts to your own situation. This model has four parts (**4-Is**): *Imagination, Ideas, Information,* and *Implementation.*

1. ***Imagination***   Use this part of the model to capture any of the thoughts that may go through your head while you are reading or hearing about a new idea or concept. Include visions and dreams that may or may not become solid ideas. Our brains constantly have imaginings running through them! Capture them on paper as you read and listen, for they are generally the best source of new ideas.

2. ***Ideas***   Ideas are more solid than imaginings. When you get an idea, you usually think: *"This is how I could do it"* or *"It could work like this!"* Write your ideas in the second section of the **Coil 4-I Planning Model**™.

3. ***Information***   When you have an idea, you usually need to gather more information to see how it might be useful in your particular situation. Write down the type of information you need and where you might find it. The information gathering phase is important, but it is also the step in the **Coil 4-I Planning Model**™ where groups or individuals have difficulty. Beware of always needing to gather more and more information before you take any action. Sometimes we spend so much time gathering information about a new idea that the idea itself gets lost, and it is never implemented!

4. ***Implementation***   This is the most important part of the model, for it is the action step where change takes place. For a new idea to have any long-term worth, you must implement it. In the **Coil 4-I Planning Model**™, write an implementation plan with target dates, and agree upon it. Modify the plan as you gather additional information.

COIL "4-I" PLANNING MODEL™

Imagination

(Visions - Possibilities - Brainstorms)

Ideas

(It could happen like this . . . This is how we could do it)

Information

(All of the things we need to find out about our situation and the possibilities we see)

Implementation

(The plan for turning our ideas into reality)

Professional Teaching Standards

The National Board for Professional Teaching Standards® founded in 1987, issued a policy statement in 1989 which has served as a basis for all of its work in developing professional standards for teachers. These have formed the basis for National Board Certification® and have functioned as a guide for school districts, states, and universities as they define high standards for professional teaching excellence. Most certainly teaching requires a broad base of both content knowledge and expertise in dealing with students, other teachers, and parents. It also requires judgment, the ability to think on one's feet, creativity, and commitment.

The policy statement of the National Board enumerates five core propositions that reflect standards of excellence in teaching. This book has both information and practical strategies teachers can use as they work toward excellence in each of the five areas. Following is a summary of the propositions and an overview of how they are discussed in this book.

1. Teachers are committed to students and their learning.

An excellent teacher finds ways to teach all students and respects differences in learning styles, learning modalities, multiple intelligences, and cultural origins. In this book, you will find chapters summarizing a variety of learning theories and showing how to offer choices in learning activities for all students. You will also find chapters on Cultural Diversity, Special Needs, and Gifted Students along with suggestions about how to best meet the individual needs of these students.

2. Teachers know the subjects they teach and how to teach those subjects to students.

Teachers who know their curriculum well can use multiple approaches to teaching the subject matter. This requires organization, interdisciplinary methodology, and real-world applications. **The Individual Lesson Plan™(ILP)** format found throughout this book gives teachers an organized structure for implementing the above. It allows for flexible teaching while incorporating the vast array of required grade-level or subject area standards. This format facilitates problem solving, higher-level thinking, and teaching for understanding.

3. Teachers are responsible for managing and monitoring student learning.

The **Individual Lesson Plan™(ILP)** format includes both Teacher Required and Student Choice activities. Choices in learning motivate students to learn. At the same time, teachers can assure the standards are being met through the required activities for all students. Chapter 1 shows how to write **ILPs™** and a way to chart and record the Student Choice activities for each student. This helps teachers keep a record of what each student is doing. It also helps organize groups of students to do a certain activity or task. The Assessment chapter gives an overview of both traditional and alternative assessments. It shows how to develop and use performance assessments, rubrics, and criteria cards both to monitor student progress and to explain this progress to students and their parents.

4. Teachers think systematically about their practice and learn from experience.

Excellent teachers are lifelong learners. They continue to learn about both their content areas and the field of teaching itself. This book is designed to facilitate teacher reflection. In addition to the **Questions to Consider** at the beginning of each chapter, this book is filled with **Teacher Reflection Pages**. These should serve as Tools for teachers to use as they examine their own teaching practices, deepen their knowledge, and incorporate new ideas and theories into their day-to-day work in the classroom.

5. Teachers are members of learning communities.

Many teachers work in isolation, rarely, if ever, collaborating in a meaningful way with other teachers. Outstanding teachers, however, work with other educators to build their own professional knowledge and expertise and to improve the overall effectiveness of their schools. This can be done by planning together in grade-level teams, in vertical teams, as a mentor for a new teacher, and/or by participating in teacher study groups. The **Individual Lesson Plan™ (ILP)** format is an excellent organizational Tool to facilitate collaborative planning. Nearly all the information in this book can be used to help mentor a new teacher and/or as the basis for a teacher study group. Collaboration also includes working in partnership with parents. Regular communication with parents and families, helping parents to understand the educational needs of their children, and assisting parents to fulfill their part in their child's education are all elements of the role of a good teacher. The Parent/Teacher Collaboration chapter is especially helpful in this regard.

Teaching is a complex, challenging, and rewarding profession. Teachers have to juggle a wide range of expectations and demands while working with a diverse student population with many different needs, interests, and abilities. It is my hope this book assists you in your professional growth as you work toward meeting high standards of excellence in the teaching profession.

Chapter 1

Teaching Creatively in the 21st Century

Questions to Consider

1. What skills do my students need to meet the changes and challenges of the 21st century?

2. What are the essential keys for teaching and learning in the 21st century?

3. What place does "choice" – teacher and student – play in learning?

4. What practical lesson planning format will help me individualize for my students?

A Time of Rapid Change

Recently I spent time in England. Everywhere I looked, I could see the new juxtaposed upon the old, evidence of centuries upon centuries of continual change. Nowhere was this more apparent than in the city of York, a city located in the industrial heartland of England, halfway between London to the South and Edinburgh to the North. The Romans settled this city in the Bronze Age in 71 A.D. Measured by American standards, it is a city with a long history and is a city that has experienced wave upon wave of change. As I walked through York, I could see Roman ruins alongside artifacts from the Saxon invasion. I could see portions of a medieval castle and was able to walk on top of the city wall built in the Middle Ages. I ate a meal in a pub built at the time of the American Revolution during the reign of King George III.

Besides these historic things, York has something very special – something that symbolized the whole idea of CHANGE for me when I saw it. In the 1980s, a group of developers decided to build a modern shopping mall in York. They chose the site carefully in an area of dilapidated buildings not far from the center of town on a street called Coppergate.

When they bulldozed buildings and started digging through layers of earth underneath, they discovered a preserved Viking village. Mud and dirt buried it beneath Coppergate for centuries. Archaeologists were called in, and they discovered layer upon layer of well-preserved archaeological artifacts. These layers, seen in an underground exhibit, are a visual representation of change. There, I looked at a vertical section of the earth. I saw physical evidence of the civilizations that had existed on that spot from the Bronze Age to the present. And yes, on top of that, there is a brand new shopping mall!

I like what they've done in York, not because I love shopping malls, but because they've looked forward as well as back. They have not destroyed the past, but they aren't stuck in it either.

So often educators take a "rear view mirror" approach. We approach the educational process the way we drive after we've been picked up on radar going too fast. We put most of our attention into looking backwards to see where we've been and then try to do the things that worked five years ago or ten years ago or even a generation ago.

In the 21st century, we need to spend less time looking out the rear view mirror and more time looking at the road ahead. Change has always been part of the human condition, but never has change been so rapid as it has been in the past few years. Sometimes change comes at such a fast pace that it's difficult to keep up with it all! The one thing that seems certain is that we will continue to experience this rapid change throughout the 21st century.

Linking School
to the 21st Century World of Work

Like other areas of life, the world of work is changing. Automated and advanced technologies are replacing many of our traditional unskilled and semiskilled workers. Additionally, manufacturing and technical jobs are being outsourced overseas. Jobs now require much more advanced knowledge and skills, but often our students do not have the relevant skills they need to work effectively now or throughout the 21st century.

Unskilled labor is no longer a valuable economic commodity, and it will become even less so in the years to come. It seems certain that in the Information Age economy, unskilled persons will become more and more unemployable.

The demand for unskilled workers is decreasing as a result of changes in technology leading to higher rates of productivity and a smaller number of workers needed to do unskilled jobs. Therefore, the long-term success of the U.S. economy requires that we have an exceptionally well-educated workforce engaged in highly skilled work that cannot be done by a machine and cannot be outsourced overseas.

Compared to other industrialized countries, the U.S. has high levels of both legal and illegal immigration. Immigrants make up approximately 30% of the labor force, and, according to the Center for Immigration Studies, they hold 35% of the unskilled jobs in the United States. Many immigrants and a number of native-born Americans have less than a high school diploma. This low educational level is a concern in our Information Age economy. Survival, economic success, and assimilation are all affected by levels of education.

Consider these facts:

According to Willard Daggett, Director of the International Center for Leadership in Education, in 1950, 60% of all jobs were unskilled and most paid a middle class wage. In 1994, 33% of all jobs were unskilled and most paid low wages. At present, few jobs require unskilled workers, and nearly all of these pay only the minimum wage. If students never experience technical reading and writing in school, never work in teams, don't develop the ability to judge quality work and effort, don't develop a work ethic, and don't understand economics and the business world, they will face problems in the world of work.

One role of education is to prepare students for this world of work. We must provide the level of education and skills required for success in our global economy and prepare our students to do the types of jobs that will be available throughout the 21st century. However, the business world expresses concern about the educational level of many students and the transfer of school-based skills into the workplace setting.

Even in traditional career fields, students need new skills. Agriculture no longer dominates the American economy as it did when the 20th century dawned. However, most of those who continue to work in agriculture in the 21st century need advanced technological, financial, and organizational skills. Manufacturing no longer requires workers who do routine tasks again and again. Those jobs are being sent overseas as we have shifted to a more flexible and automated manufacturing system. The result is that workers who continue in the manufacturing sector need technological skills and the ability to process information symbolically, mostly via computers. They also need advanced reading and language skills and the ability to think critically.

Skilled workers in the 21st century now deal mostly with services and information. To do this, they need to understand advanced technological applications involving the use of math, language, and thinking skills. Knowledge of statistics, logic, probability, measurement systems, and applied physics are also important. Because businesses need to communicate with customers regularly, these same workers need to express themselves well, organize information and activities, and do a great deal of technical reading and writing.

Furthermore, most 21st century jobs require the ability to work well in task-oriented groups or teams and to solve problems critically and creatively. However, for the most part, schools teach students to work independently, while the world of work needs workers who know how to work interdependently with one another. Because today's students will be part of a global economy and workplace, this interdependence also involves the ability to understand people from a variety of cultures who may have different cultural values and norms.

Other Needs of 21st Century Students

As important as they are, future jobs and the world of work should not be our only considerations as we think of the needs of 21st century students. Job preparation is only one of the many needs of our students. We also must consider their abilities to be good citizens, physically fit persons, contributing family members, lifelong learners, appreciators of the arts, history, and culture, and caring, compassionate people. The teacher holds the key to developing these more intangible educational outcomes.

Four Keys for Teaching in the 21st Century

Four essential keys for successful teaching and learning in the 21st century are **Flexibility, Resources, Choices,** and **Planning**. Each of these Key ideas moves away from the 19th and 20th century Industrial Age mode of everyone learning and doing the same thing at the same time to the Information Age model of individualized lifelong learning. If we want our children to develop abilities in higher-level thinking, teachers must model teaching in ways that enhance critical and creative thought.

➔ Flexibility

Flexible teachers are risk takers who are willing to make changes and try new ideas. We can no longer teach by giving all students the same assignment and expecting them to complete it simultaneously with equal accuracy and quality. A "one size fits all" lesson usually fits no one!

Flexibility implies that all students will not, together in a lockstep fashion, always do classroom activities and assignments chosen by the teacher. Flexibility means acknowledging that it will take some students a long time to learn an idea or skill while other students already know it before you begin the lesson. And it means making provisions for these differing ability levels and pacing within your classroom.

Flexible teachers must be willing to give up some of their lecture time and use texts and workbooks as just one of many classroom resources. A flexible teacher realizes that doing a series of questions at the end of the chapter does not meet most students' learning needs.

Flexibility means allowing for differences in:

- Learning styles

- Learning modalities

- Strengths/weaknesses in the multiple intelligences

- Pace of learning and lesson presentation

- Time needed to complete a task

- Student interests

- Ability levels

→ Resources

Through technology many of our students can now access new information with the press of a button. For example, a generation ago students who were assigned to write a report on the explorations of Christopher Columbus would get several books, research the information, and write the report by hand. Now they can access a multitude of sources on CD ROM and the Internet, unthinkingly cut and paste the information electronically, press a computer key, and print out their reports. Present-day assignments **must** require much more thinking than that!

Due to technological advances and the greater availability of information from a multitude of sources, students have an unlimited access to knowledge. No longer is a teacher or the textbook the only resource for knowledge and information. The role of the teacher is changing, with the teacher becoming a model of lifelong learning for his or her students. Thus, students and their teachers are all fellow learners who can share resources, find new information, and analyze this information together.

Yet, technology can also drown us in a flood of information. Our students can end up spending all their time sifting through the vast amount of information that is readily available, having difficulty knowing what information is reliable and what is not.

Teachers, too, may feel as if they are drowning. They have limited instructional time and a multitude of standards to cover. When the curriculum is merely added to with more and more "stuff," teachers struggle and realize they cannot do it all. There needs to be another approach.

With such a huge curriculum, teachers need to understand that they do not have to know all the answers. This is an advantage educationally, because when teachers don't know the answers, they can model what learning is all about. Teachers become learners as well as their students, assuming the role of co-learner in the classroom. In the 21st century, this role for teachers is becoming a necessity.

With so much knowledge and information, how do we know what should be taught? One approach, called "selective abandonment" by Art Costa, is to remove outdated, irrelevant, and unnecessary information from the curriculum. Many educators have a large number of resources that are not only outdated but also don't meet today's standards. Teachers need to sort through and re-evaluate their resources regularly. Consider this cleaning out your mental file cabinet!

Even when they do this, most teachers are overwhelmed at all they are required to teach. One of the best approaches to flexible teaching is to look at your standards, then integrate and connect the curriculum through standards-based thematic interdisciplinary units. The Tools presented in this book will help you do this.

→ **Choices**

Student Choices / Student-Directed Learning

Choices are everywhere. Consider an average day for eleven-year-old Richard. He downloads the music he likes onto his ipod choosing from an unlimited selection. Next, he strolls through the mall looking for a new shirt and can choose from the hundreds of different shirts on the clothing racks in every store he passes. Later he goes to the grocery store with his mom. He doesn't even think about the number of cereals or soft drinks he chooses from as he fills the shopping cart with his favorite foods. Later, he does an Internet search on a topic and finds 8,964 web sites! Choices fill our students' everyday lives.

Choice affects education as it does all other goods and services in our advanced modern economy. Schools in the 21st century must market themselves and attempt to satisfy the expectations of their clients – the parents and students. Within the classroom, students need to have choices in their learning as well. Teachers should structure many choices into each student's day. Why is this important? Students feel a sense of ownership in the tasks they do when teachers give choices in classroom assignments. When teachers include the element of choice in learning experiences, they increase the chances that students will achieve optimal learning.

As you plan units, lessons, and learning activities for your students ask yourself these questions:
- ❑ What standards are my students working on?
- ❑ Why am I teaching this?
- ❑ Why is it important for my students to do this activity?
- ❑ How can I eliminate some redundant or rote activities and still meet my standards and objectives?
- ❑ How can I structure this unit or lesson in such a way to give my students choices?

These questions will help you plan the approach you take in structuring learning activities in your classroom. It is important to remember that what goes on in the classroom affects what students learn. This is the area where teachers have the most control. One way to help students progress in learning the standards is to offer standards-based choices in their learning activities.

Types of Student Choices

For most students, there have been few times in their school lives that teachers have allowed them to make choices in their learning. Our goal should be to increase their options for learning. Constructive choices for students can come in all shapes and sizes. Students should be able to choose which tasks to complete to accomplish goals and meet the mandated standards. The teacher needs to offer several choices for students by varying the structure of the curriculum, classroom activities, and projects.

The number and types of student choices depend on the teacher's comfort level with a variety of instructional approaches. Students should be able to choose several different approaches for the same learning outcome. Give them choices in types of activities, timing, and/or ways to learn. These choices must be real choices, with no hidden preference by the teacher. Begin with a limited number of choices. Eventually, give students who become adept at making choices for their own learning the opportunity to develop their own choices and alternatives.

Giving students choices is risky. Student-directed learning requires a tremendous shift in the way teachers think and how they plan. **Teachers have to be flexible because once students make choices, they don't always make the choices or go in directions teachers think they should. Because of this, it is important to give students choices with which you are comfortable.**

A word of caution: We don't want to give our students so much choice that they end up learning nothing. The role of the teacher is to plan and structure the curriculum to meet essential outcomes and required grade-level standards. Teachers should always focus on leading students to achieve excellence. For these reasons, the teacher must be the one to outline the parameters and opportunities for choice.

Advantages of Student Choices

Allowing students to direct their own learning has several advantages:

- ❑ Students learn good decision-making skills.
- ❑ Students learn to organize and take responsibility for their own learning.
- ❑ Students can and do take ownership of their learning.
- ❑ The curriculum can be adapted to meet student interests.
- ❑ Lessons are more meaningful, and students become personally involved in them.
- ❑ Teachers are able to narrow the focus of curriculum units.

The best way to give students choices is to allow them choices within a range of potential activities. A student's learning style, learning modality, individual interests, and use of the multiple intelligences determines the student choices in meeting the objectives.

An essential classroom rule when giving students choices in their learning activities is the following:

The one choice you never have is the choice to do nothing.

Teacher Choices/Teacher-Directed Learning

In a classroom where students direct their own learning by making choices in curricular activities, the teacher becomes valuable as an experienced guide in the process of learning. Teachers need to take on the role of guides in the classroom because deciding what content should be learned or studied is very difficult. Students need guidance to assess what they need to learn so they can solve a problem or complete a project.

Providing such guidance can prove challenging for teachers who must also ensure that students meet academic objectives and standards established by school districts or states. Many states list objectives in the state's curriculum framework and give students standardized tests to make sure they meet these standards. Severe penalties can result if students fail to make adequate yearly progress (AYP) on standardized tests.

A landmark piece of Federal legislation called the *No Child Left Behind Act (NCLB)* went into effect in 2002. This law requires yearly testing of all students in grades 3-8 in language arts, reading, math, and science. It also requires testing of all students once in grades 10-12. The tests are aligned to the state standards and are intended to show adequate yearly progress (AYP) for all children. The goal is to have all children in American public schools at a proficient level by 2014.

Because of this, one valid concern in giving students choices in their leaning is that standards will not be met because there will be too many gaps in students' knowledge. Teachers or their superiors may feel that the only way to ensure that this does not happen is to have everyone cover certain books, topics, or assignments. Yet meeting standards can work hand-in-hand with student-directed learning when teachers guide students in making choices. The choice comes in HOW to meet the standards, not in whether or not the standards will be met.

Many teachers are frustrated and confused, wanting to be flexible and give students choices in their learning activities yet feeling pressure to make sure students meet district or statewide standards. These two ideas do not have to be mutually exclusive, but accomplishing both takes **planning**!

➜ Planning

While agreeing in principle that curriculum and instruction should be differentiated and that learning should be flexible and provide choices, many teachers have done little in these areas because of the vast amount of planning they perceive it requires. In fact, it does take planning to reach differing ability levels and a variety of interest areas.

Look at the **Individual Lesson Plan™ (ILP)** format on page 22. It is an effective, easy-to-use Tool for lesson planning that offers you flexibility. Its structure provides for Student Choices, yet it also allows you to include required Teacher Choice learning activities for all students. This format is one of several **Individual Lesson Plan™ (ILP)** formats in this book. In the remaining portion of this chapter and in several subsequent chapters, you will discover how you can use this Tool to plan choices in learning for your students.

How to Begin

Some teachers like to use interdisciplinary thematic units, while others prefer more content or subject-based units. An **interdisciplinary thematic unit** uses a topic or concept as a theme and infuses this theme into a number of different content areas. A **content-based** or **subject-based unit** may touch on other disciplines, but its focus is on one subject area. You can use the **Individual Lesson Plan™ (ILP)** format with both.

Begin planning your unit by generating a list of ideas, broad unit questions, objectives, and a list of standards you intend to cover. (The Planner is found on page 18.) Then brainstorm as many activities as possible that students could do to accomplish these standards and objectives. Collaborate with other teachers as you gather ideas for activities and look at a variety of resources about the topic. Ask your students what they already know or are interested in about the topic or subject on which you will focus. Brainstorming potential unit activities with your students can lead to more student motivation and can serve as one type of pre-assessment.

After you have completed this initial planning, use the **ILP™** format to structure your unit. Look at the list of questions, standards, and student activities for a unit on **Inventors and Inventions** on page 19. Then see how these fit into the **ILP™** format on page 21.

The checklist on page 17 gives you step-by-step guidelines for developing an **ILP™** unit.

Steps to Develop an ILP™ *

____ 1. Decide on a major theme or topic for the unit.

____ 2. Generate a unit rationale, a broad list of essential questions, objectives, and outcomes that would include several subject areas, and the enduring understandings you hope will come out of the unit.

____ 3. Correlate unit objectives and outcomes with state standards in several subject areas.

____ 4. Brainstorm a list of possible unit activities.

____ 5. Classify each activity according to learning modalities, learning styles, Bloom's Taxonomy, and/or multiple intelligences.

____ 6. Decide which will be Student Choice activities and which will be required of all students.

____ 7. Include one independent activity in the activities required of all students. This will be the activity all students can work on while you are meeting with small groups of students and discussing their Student Choice activities.

____ 8. Use the **Individual Lesson Plan™ (ILP)** format to organize your unit activities.

____ 9. Write all Student Choice activities in consecutive numerical order for easy reference. This way, you can keep a record of which students have chosen which activity just by recording the number of the activity.

____ 10. Find or develop resources and materials needed for the unit.

____ 11. Develop assessments to assess unit objectives, outcomes, and standards. You could develop complete rubrics, mini-rubrics, tests or quizzes, observation logs, charts, and a host of other assessment instruments.

____ 12. Develop daily lesson plans based on your unit plan.

* (From *Activities and Assessments for the Differentiated Classroom* by Carolyn Coil. Pieces of Learning, 2004.)

"When we do the best that we can, we never know what miracle is wrought in our life or in the life of another."
Helen Keller

Planner for Curriculum Activities

Topic or Theme_____

What do I want my students to know about this topic? What are the essential questions we want to answer? What are the Big Ideas?

- _____
- _____
- _____
- _____

What state standards are we working to meet?

- _____
- _____
- _____
- _____
- _____

Possible Student Activities	Product/Performance	LM/LS/Bloom/MI
1. _____	_____	_____
2. _____	_____	_____
3. _____	_____	_____
4. _____	_____	_____
5. _____	_____	_____
6. _____	_____	_____
7. _____	_____	_____
8. _____	_____	_____
9. _____	_____	_____
10. _____	_____	_____
11. _____	_____	_____
12. _____	_____	_____

Sample Planner for an ILP™ Unit

(Topic or Theme)   Inventors and Inventions

What do I want my students to know about this topic? What are the essential questions we want to answer? What are the Big Ideas?

- How do inventions change and develop over time?
- How do inventions affect people's lives?
- What should I know about famous inventors and significant inventions?
- How does a person invent something?
- **What state standards are we working to meet?**
- Inquire and conduct research using a variety of sources.
- Interpret and use graphic sources of information: charts, graphs, and time lines.
- Know that past events affect present and future events.
- Understand how people help shape the community, state, and nation.
- Understand how science and technology have affected the past and the present.

Possible Student Activities	Product/Performance	LM//LS/Bloom/MI
1. Write and perform a song about an invention	song	verbal, kinesthetic, musical synthesis
2. Paint mural of inventions	mural	visual, kinesthetic, application
3. Make a time line showing the development of a specific invention	time line	visual, mathematical/logical comprehension
4. Create a collage of 19th or 20th century inventions	collage	visual, kinesthetic, knowledge
5. Research the life of a famous inventor. Do a presentation.	presentation	technological, comprehension
6. Do a skit showing changes brought about by a specific invention	skit	verbal, kinesthetic, analysis
7. Pretend you are an invention. Act out what you are.	dramatic action	kinesthetic, intrapersonal synthesis
8. Make a chart showing the % of times per day you use inventions	chart	visual, logical/mathematical application
9. Develop a crossword puzzle of inventions	crossword puzzle	verbal, visual, comprehension
10. Write a letter to the editor giving your views about an invention	letter to the editor	verbal, evaluation
11. Design your car of the future and explain how it works	design & explanation	visual, verbal, synthesis
12. Do a survey to see what inventions people own	survey	verbal, mathematical/logical knowledge

© Carolyn Coil

Using the Individual Lesson Plan™ (ILP) Format

After you have completed this initial planning of your unit, you should be ready to use the **Individual Lesson Plan**™ **(ILP)** format. Decide first which activities you want all of your students to do. The upper right quadrant of the ILP is for these activities. List these activities in the first block labeled **Required Activities - Teacher's Choice**. The products and performances resulting from completing these activities along with the criteria for assessment will be listed in the two blocks on the right. Look at an example from the *Inventors and Inventions* unit:

Required Activities Teacher's Choice	Product/Performance	Assessment
1. Read the textbook information about inventions in both the social studies and science books. Make a Compare / Contrast chart showing the information.	1. Compare/Contrast Chart *(Due date recorded here)*	1. Appropriate visual Correct facts Deductive reasoning Organization
2. Listen to a talk by a local inventor. Write a reaction paper.	2. Reaction paper *(Due date recorded here)*	2. Facts & opinions clearly stated Sentence structure
3. Take a final test about Inventors & Inventions.	3. Test answers *(Due date recorded here)*	3. Accurate answers Numerical score

In addition to outlining the Teacher Required activities for all students, the **Individual Lesson Plan**™ **(ILP)** format also provides a structured method whereby students can make choices in their learning activities. It gives teachers the flexibility to individualize and serve a variety of subject areas, learning styles, learning modalities, taxonomy levels and/or ability levels. Look at one set of Student Choice activities from the *Inventors and Inventions* unit found on the next page. In this example the Student Choices are organized according to subject areas.

If you look at the blank Subject Activities **Individual Lesson Plan**™**(ILP)** format on page 22 you will see there are blocks indicating each subject area. Use these for Student Choice activities. Other versions of the **Individual Student Lesson Plan**™**(ILP)** format found in upcoming chapters of this book have one block for each of four learning styles (pages 37-38), four learning modalities (pages 53-54), six Bloom's Taxonomy levels (pages 63-64) , four higher Bloom's Taxonomy levels (pages 65-66), and eight multiple intelligences (pages 83-84). In general, two or three activity choices should be listed in each block for students in grade 4 - 12. Generally do not have more than twelve Student Choice activities on the **ILP**™. Younger students do better with even fewer choices. See page 25 for more information about using the **ILP**™ with these students.

INDIVIDUAL LESSON PLAN - Subject Activities

Required Activities — Teacher's Choice

1. Read the textbook information about inventions in both the social studies and science books. Make a Compare/Contrast chart showing the information.

2. Listen to a talk by a local inventor. Write a reaction paper.

3. Take a final test about Inventors & Inventions.

Product/Performance Required

1. Compare/Contrast chart
   (Due date recorded here)

2. Reaction Paper
   (Due Date recorded here)

3. Test answers
   (Due Date recorded here)

Assessment — Required Activities

1. Appropriate visual
   Correct facts
   Deductive reasoning
   Organization

2. Facts & opinions clearly stated
   Sentence structure

3. Accurate answers
   Numerical score

Standards

Optional Student-Parent Cooperative Activity

(11) Calculate the percentage of times per day you use 10 inventions.

Product/Performance Student Choice

Due Date Student Choice

Student Choices in Ways to Learn

Science

Social Studies

Performing Arts

Language Arts

Visual Arts

Math

ACTIVITIES - STUDENT CHOICES

Science

1. Design your car of the future. Explain how it would work.

2. Make a time line showing the stages in the development of an invention of your choice.

Language Arts

7. Write a letter to the editor thanking Gutenberg for inventing the printing press.

8. Make a crossword puzzle of inventions.

Social Studies

3. Research the life of a famous inventor. Share your information with your class in a creative way.

4. Do a skit showing the changes brought about by a specific invention.

Visual Arts

9. Create a collage of 19th century or 20th century inventions.

10. With a group of classmates, paint a mural of inventions.

Performing Arts

5. Pretend you are an invention. Act out what you are. Your classmates are allowed 20 questions to guess what you are.

6. Write and perform a song about an invention.

Math

11. Calculate the % of time per day that you use any 10 inventions. Make a chart showing results.

12. Survey your neighborhood to see what cars people own. Show car ownership on a graph.

INDIVIDUAL LESSON PLAN - Subject Activities

Assessment Required Activities	Product/Performance Required	Required Activities Teacher's Choice

Standards		

Due Date Student Choice	Product/Performance Student Choice	Optional Student-Parent Cooperative Activity

Student Choices in Ways to Learn

Science _____

Social Studies _____

Performing Arts _____

Language Arts _____

Visual Arts _____

Math _____

ACTIVITIES - STUDENT CHOICES

Language Arts	Visual Arts	Math

Science	Social Studies	Performing Arts

 CLC0378 Pieces of Learning

How Student Choice Can Be Structured and Implemented

The **Individual Lesson Plan**™ (ILP) format allows the teacher to have some control over the activities the students are completing both by requiring Teacher Choice activities and by the way in which the Student Choice activities are implemented. For example, students could be told to choose two activities from one of the Student Choice blocks and one from another. Or one from each block, or two from two different blocks. It is up to each teacher to decide how to structure the choices.

When using the **Individual Lesson Plan**™ (ILP) format there also needs to be some type of a time line or schedule so that students, their parents, and the teacher know the date various products and assignments must be turned in. Review due dates for the required activities and have the students write the dates as shown on page 21.

Give each student a copy of the **Individual Lesson Plan**™ (ILP) format with the Teacher's Choice and Student Choice activities already listed (page 21). When the new unit is introduced, review all the activities and choices with the entire class. Next, students make their choices of activities by writing the number for each activity on the line in the center block. Then students write on the chart what products and/or performances are required for each activity that they have chosen (page 24). The criteria for assessing each Student Choice activity is listed on the back of the ILP. For more on assessment, see Chapter 6. The **Individual Lesson Plan**™ (ILP) format for **Inventors and Inventions** showing how Student Choices are indicated is on page 24. Use the reproducible blank format with Student Choices by subject area on page 22 to design your own units.

Using the ILP™ for Sub-topics within a Unit of Study

Sometimes teachers are required to teach units of study with a large amount of knowledge all students need to master. In this case, divide the topic of study into sub-topics, and use each sub-topic as a category for Student Choice activities on the **ILP**™. In this way, all students will address the required content but may learn it in different ways.

Using the Individual Lesson™ Plan (ILP) Format
in a Mixed Ability Classroom

In a mixed ability classroom, use this format for everyone. Structure it with easier choices and more difficult choices, or if you prefer that all students have the same choices, differentiate the quality, level, and expectations for the products depending on the ability level of each child. Teacher guidance is needed to make sure students make appropriate choices and that they know how to approach the task once the choice is made. See page 118 about developing Questivities™ to learn more about guiding and extending students' thinking after they have chosen an activity. Using Questivities™ is an excellent strategy for challenging high-ability students.

Gifted and high-ability students often finish their work before others in the class. When this happens while they are working on activities from the **Individual Lesson Plan**™ (ILP) format, they do not have to wait for others to finish, nor do they have to do "busy work." They can either choose an additional activity from the choices in the **ILP**™ or create a new activity about the topic as an additional choice.

INDIVIDUAL LESSON PLAN - Subject Activities

ACTIVITIES - STUDENT CHOICES

Science

1. Design your car of the future. Explain how it would work.

2. Make a time line showing the stages in the development of an invention of your choice.

Social Studies

3. Research the life of a famous inventor. Share your information with your class in a creative way.

4. Do a skit showing the changes brought about by a specific invention.

Performing Arts

5. Pretend you are an invention. Act out what you are. Your classmates are allowed 20 questions to guess what you are.

6. Write and perform a song about an invention.

Language Arts

7. Write a letter to the editor thanking Gutenberg for inventing the printing press.

8. Make a crossword puzzle of inventions.

Visual Arts

9. Create a collage of 19th century or 20th century inventions.

10. With a group of classmates, paint a mural of inventions.

Math

11. Calculate the % of time per day that you use any 10 inventions. Make a chart showing results.

12. Survey your neighborhood to see what cars people own. Show car ownership on a graph.

Required Activities — Teacher's Choice

1. Read the textbook information about inventions in both the social studies and science books. Make a Compare/Contrast chart showing the information.

2. Listen to a talk by a local inventor. Write a reaction paper.

3. Take a final test about Inventors & Inventions.

Optional Student-Parent Cooperative Activity

(11) Calculate the percentage of times per day you use 10 inventions.

Student Choices in Ways to Learn

Science
2

Social Studies
4

Performing Arts
6

Language Arts
8

Visual Arts
10

Math
12

Product/Performance Required

1. Compare/Contrast chart
(Due date recorded here)

2. Reaction Paper
(Due Date recorded here)

3. Test answers
(Due Date recorded here)

Product/Performance Student Choice

2. Time line

4. Skit

6. Song

8. Crossword Puzzle

10. Mural

12. Graph

Assessment — Required Activities

1. Appropriate visual
Correct facts
Deductive reasoning
Organization

2. Facts & opinions clearly stated
Sentence structure

3. Accurate answers
Numerical score

Standards

Due Date — Student Choice

(Due date recorded here)

Adapting the Individual Lesson Plan™ (ILP) Format for Primary Students

Primary students need to learn to make choices, but the choices need to be fewer and completed over a shorter period of time. Use a bulletin board to show Student Choices and have students use sticky notes to put their names on the bulletin board next to the activities they choose. A good way to begin is to have a total of four Student Choice activities, and have each student choose one.

Visual	**Kinesthetic**
Technological	**Auditory/Verbal**

Using the Optional Student-Parent Cooperative Activity

Many parents become interested in their child's school projects. To capture this interest and use it in a positive way, you may allow your students to choose one activity to do with their parents. This not only involves the parents in classroom activities, it also helps them be models of lifelong learners for their children. Additionally, for overly zealous parents who always want to help their child, this provides an outlet to do it!

Including Standards
on the Individual Lesson Plan™ (ILP) Format

The **ILP**™ form has a place to indicate the standards addressed in the unit of study. Most units will be interdisciplinary and therefore may address standards in a number of different areas. Use the numbers of your state standards as a quick reference.

Using the Individual Lesson Plan™ (ILP) Format
to Form Student Groups

Use an Activity Chart to record the activities that each of your students choose. (See sample on page 27.) Each Student Choice activity is numbered and can be easily checked off beside the student's name. When all the Student Choices have been recorded on this chart, you have a visual organizer that you can use to group students according to the activities they choose. Some of the activities may need to be done in a group (such as a skit) but even students doing individual activities will benefit by planning, discussing, and brainstorming with others who are doing the same activity. Meet with each of these groups separately to go over assessment criteria, establish due dates, and talk about the activities. My rule is that once students have told me their choices and these have been recorded on the Activity Chart, they must stick with this choice and cannot change their minds. This helps students choose more carefully and teaches important lessons in making a commitment, taking responsibility, and persisting when a task is more difficult than anticipated.

Reflections

* 21st Century students will need a multiplicity of new skills to meet the needs and demands of a rapidly changing world.

* Four essential keys for teaching and learning in the 21st century are *flexibility, resources, choices*, and *planning*.

* We need to offer opportunities for students to make choices and direct their own learning in combination with required Teacher's Choice learning activities.

* The **Individual Lesson Plan™ (ILP)** format provides a structure for planning and implementing both types of learning activities.

Activity Chart
Sample

Student Choice Activities

Students' Names	1	2	3	4	5	6	7	8	9	10	11	12
Alicia		✔							✔			
Carlos			✔			✔						
Danielle	✔				✔							
Evan			✔				✔					
Edwardo				✔					✔			
Gina			✔									✔
Heather				✔		✔						
Jim				✔							✔	
Kara	✔											✔
Maria			✔						✔			
Mark				✔			✔					
Nathan	✔				✔							
Ophra							✔					✔
Paul		✔			✔							
Pedro				✔				✔				
Quintan							✔					✔
Rachel				✔					✔			
Rusty					✔	✔						
Sarah	✔			✔								
Taneka		✔					✔					
Tom	✔			✔								

This group of students was instructed to make 2 choices from the 12 Student Choice activities available. Each child's choices are recorded.

Students who chose 4 and 10, group activities, are grouped together to work on their activities. Groups of students for each choice meet with the teacher to review assessment criteria.

Activity Chart

Student Choice Activities

Students' Names	1	2	3	4	5	6	7	8	9	10	11	12

Notes

Chapter 2
Learning Styles

Questions to Consider

1. What do learning styles indicate?

2. What are four basic learning styles?

3. Why is it important for students to know their strong and weak styles?

4. How can I accommodate all learning styles into the curriculum?

Teachers in the 21st century need working knowledge of basic learning styles. It is important to know about these styles and be able to work with each so that you can plan your lessons taking each style into account. In the past, good teachers have intuitively used a variety of teaching styles. With the requirements for adequate yearly progress (AYP) from all students coupled with the challenges of teaching students from a variety of cultures, and students with diverse needs, we must be more intentional about how we are teaching. We no longer have the luxury of ignoring or refusing to teach to any of these styles.

Successful adults can generally work in any learning style, but most have a style of preference and strength. In the same way, it is equally important for you to help your students to identify their strong and weak style(s). Over time, assist them in becoming adept at working in all styles. It would not be good teaching practice to identify the preferred learning style for each of our students and then restrict them to that style! When students are encouraged to develop a learning style they previously considered weak, rather than detracting from other areas, the development seems to create a synergistic effect in which all areas of mental performance improve.

Learning styles indicate the ways in which people process information. Dr. Anthony Gregorc has identified four basic learning styles. They are:

Concrete Sequential   Abstract Sequential   Concrete Random   Abstract Random

Both **concrete** styles deal with objects and concrete, hands-on, experiential learning.
Both **abstract** styles deal with more theoretical thinking apart from one object or example.
Both **sequential** styles deal with processing information in a linear, orderly fashion.
Both **random** styles deal with processing information in no particular order, in a more haphazard, non-uniform way.

Research studies by Griggs & Dunn (1998) show a positive relationship between academic achievement, beneficial attitudes, desirable classroom behavior, and the accommodation of students' learning style preferences in the classroom. Their studies also show that some learning styles are developmental, and many people's styles change as they grow older. Knowing about learning styles is important because they give us direction and structure for developing effective teaching strategies. Thus, it is important for you to discover the learning styles of your students. As you read the next several pages, think about your own students. Which students fit the descriptions of each learning style?

The Concrete Sequential Learning Style

Jana is in the 4th grade and is considered an excellent student. She has her school supplies on the first day of school and generally keeps them intact all year. She writes down her assignments, turns them in on time, and (to the chagrin of other students) reminds the teacher when they are due. Her outlines are always done in sequential order, with the proper Roman numerals and letters. However, she is not an imaginative student and seems to lack creativity. She dislikes teachers who skip around in the book or who don't teach in a logical order. Her preferred learning style is concrete sequential.

This student likes to:

- read and follow directions. For example, this student will read the directions before touching an electronic device and will follow the recipe exactly when cooking something.

- take notes, make charts, and create outlines. This student is the one other students turn to for the notes to study before a major test.

- participate in "hands-on" experiences, including pencil and paper exercises. As the name of this learning style suggests, this student likes to work with concrete things and does well with written work, hands-on projects, and assignments involving specific products.

- have an organized teacher. This student will still have the syllabus on the last day of the term and will know if you've stuck to it!

- always know the grading system. This student can tell you exactly what grades he or she has made on each assignment since the beginning of the grading period. If the teacher forgets to return a set of papers, this student will remind her to do it.

Concrete Sequential students enjoy learning activities and products such as the following:

- ❑ Outlines
- ❑ Note taking
- ❑ Charts
- ❑ Graphs
- ❑ Following rubrics and checklists
- ❑ Story boards
- ❑ Comic Strips
- ❑ Comic Books

> **Schools usually reward concrete sequential students.**

The Abstract Sequential Learning Style

Colin, an 11th grader, has always liked to read. He began reading when he was three, and it seems he has had a book in his hands ever since! By the time he was in first grade he was reading at a fourth grade level. He is very good at math and science and looks at everything logically. Colin can win arguments with anyone if only logic is involved. His intuitive and social skills are not as well developed. He has a hard time with his peers, and some of the other kids call him a 'nerd.' He has a crush on an 11th grade girl and has thought through all the steps to ask her to the prom. He's sure if he approaches this situation in a logical, step-by-step fashion she will go to the prom with him.

This student likes to:

- read different kinds of books. This student usually has a library book to read when an assignment is finished or when he or she is bored with assigned schoolwork. Because of this preference for reading, this student generally has working knowledge in a variety of areas.

- listen to audio tapes, compact disks, and lectures, see videos, films, and slides, and work on the computer and other electronic learning tools. Generally, this is the student who is quite technologically oriented and may know more about the computer than the teacher does!

- help other students understand the subject matter or what they've read and is usually willing to tutor a classmate or a group of younger students. On the other hand, this student is not very good at "small talk" when the topic is not defined.

- find THE answer to a problem and is uncomfortable with open-ended questions, multiple answers, and possibilities. This student sees no reason to have brainstorming sessions that accept all answers, and often doesn't see the purpose in "What would happen if . . ." questions. He or she may object to such a question asking, "But what actually did happen? Isn't that what is important?"

- look at things logically, even in situations where a logical solution is not necessarily the best one or does not solve the problem.

Abstract Sequential students enjoy learning activities and products such as the following:

- ❑ Logic puzzles
- ❑ Computer activities
- ❑ Listening to lectures
- ❑ Explaining how something works
- ❑ Written or oral book reports
- ❑ Tutoring classmates
- ❑ Producing audio tapes

> **Abstract sequential students usually do very well academically, though they may have problems with social skills. Their intuitive and emotional skills are often weak.**

The Concrete Random Learning Style

Thirteen-year-old Paul cheered and clapped when his history teacher said the class had a choice between doing either a written report or a project on the same topic covered in the thematic unit. As far as Paul was concerned, doing a project wasn't like doing 'real' school work at all. When the teacher asked the class to brainstorm project ideas, Paul's hand was constantly in the air. By the end of class, he was already thinking of how he could build a replica of a pioneer settlement using some twigs and branches he knew were in the woods behind his house. "I wish I could do this kind of stuff in all my classes," he thought to himself.

This student likes to:

- complete a product for a classroom assignment. Somehow this doesn't seem to be "work" like a written paper or a set of questions to be answered at the end of a chapter. This student will do an excellent job with a hands-on project, but unlike the concrete sequential student, may not turn it in on time.

- brainstorm creative ideas. This student is never worried about what the "right" answer is. Whether in a large or small group, this student will contribute many ideas in almost any brainstorming activity.

- take risks. Concrete random students will volunteer for anything, even if they do not know what it will involve, especially if it will get them out of class. Often, these students will get into trouble because of risk-taking behavior!

- do things by trial and error. Don't give this student the directions and expect him to follow them! Instead, he will try different possibilities until he discovers a way of doing something that works best for him.

- solve problems alone. Group work is not these students' favorite. They would rather figure out the problem on their own, often by "fooling around" with concrete objects until something works out correctly.

- avoid IQ and achievement tests. These students normally do not do very well on multiple choice, true/false, or other types of objective tests. Because they can see multiple possibilities, even "wrong" answers may seem defensible to them. Essay and short answer tests, portfolio and alternative assessments, or class projects suit these students much better.

Concrete Random students enjoy learning activities and products such as the following:

- ❑ Constructing models
- ❑ Brainstorming
- ❑ Dissecting anything
- ❑ Collages
- ❑ Inventing new games
- ❑ Taking notes using concept maps or webs
- ❑ Science experiments

> **Schools traditionally have more trouble programming for students with random learning styles.**

The Abstract Random Learning Style

Taneka, a 6th grader, has lots of friends and loves to talk. She enjoys her friends at school, and when she gets home from school the phone calls start. Her dad teases her, saying her cell phone is growing out of her ear! At school her talking bothers some of her teachers so they sit her in the front of the classroom, thinking this may keep her from talking. But most of the time she just turns around and talks anyway. Taneka likes to read and can tell you the titles of several favorite books. Usually she reads the first few chapters and then skims over the rest, just getting the main ideas. She is likable, popular, and has excellent leadership skills.

This student likes to:

- listen to, learn from, and respond to their classmates. They thrive on class discussions and wish that the teacher would structure class like a large discussion group all the time. Even when someone tries to "get the teacher off the subject" the abstract random learner learns from whatever he or she hears.

- work in groups. These are the students who benefit most from cooperative learning and other forms of group work. Often they will become the natural leaders in small groups and can make everyone feel included.

- read short reading assignments. They like to read, but find it hard to sit still long enough to read long books. Lots of shorter reading assignments suit them better.

- use emotions and intuition. Often these students come up with the right answer but can't tell you the logical steps of how they got it. Their thought processes are intuitive, not logical.

- have lots of things going on at once. They are the "jugglers" and think that the more things they do the better. They take on lots of new things but are not as good at following through over a long period of time.

Abstract Random students enjoy learning activities and products such as the following:

- ❏ Organizing a panel discussion
- ❏ Debates
- ❏ Cooperative Learning projects
- ❏ Interviews
- ❏ Class discussions
- ❏ Comparing and contrasting characters in different stories
- ❏ Student-led conferences with parents

> **These are the students who are always talking.**

Learning Styles

Teacher Reflection Page

List the names of one or more of your students and descriptive traits of each that fit each learning style.

Concrete Sequential

Abstract Sequential

Concrete Random

Abstract Random

Mixture of learning styles

Learning Styles

Classroom Activities

Which learning style(s) do you incorporate in your classroom?

1. List several activities you have done in your class in the past two or three weeks. Indicate the learning style(s) they are most suited for.

I. Activity:

Learning style(s):

II. Activity:

Learning style(s):

III. Activity:

Learning style(s):

IV. Activity:

Learning style(s):

2. Which style(s) do most of your classroom activities lend themselves to?

3. Which style(s) are most difficult for you to work with?

Using the Individual Lesson Plan™ (ILP) Format
to Plan Units
Incorporating Learning Styles

After you have done the initial planning of your unit (see page 18), decide which activities you want all of your students to do. As in the previous chapter, list these activities in the block in the center of the **Individual Lesson Plan™ (ILP)** format labeled **Required Activities - Teacher's Choice.** List the products that will be turned in as a result of doing these activities and criteria for assessment in the two blocks on the right.

Now look at the remainder of the activities you listed. These will become your **Student Choice Activities**. Review the characteristics for each learning style. Decide which activities are appropriate for each learning style. Using a form similar to the one on the preceding page (*Classroom Activities*) may be helpful in making this determination. If you do not have enough activities for a particular learning style, look again at your unit objectives and standards. How could you design learning activities for each learning style that would meet the objectives and standards? If you run out of ideas, have your students or a colleague brainstorm with you. Also, refer to pages 30-33 and 232-233 for additional ideas.

On the next page is the **Individual Lesson Plan™ (ILP)** with the Student Choices based on Learning Styles.

One of the activities for the **Concrete Sequential** learner is to make a time line showing famous inventions. This activity works well with the type of learner who likes to make charts and outlines. An activity appropriate for the **Abstract Sequential** learning style is to read a biography about a famous inventor and give an oral report to the class, because this is the type of student who loves to read and share this knowledge with other students. For the **Concrete Random** student, an appropriate activity is to construct a model of a new invention. This type of student likes doing "hands-on" projects. Finally, for the **Abstract Random** student, one of the activities is to choose an important invention and debate its merits with a classmate. This is the learning style that likes to learn from and respond to other students in the class.

A reproducible blank form with student choices by learning styles is on page 38. Use this to design your own units.

INDIVIDUAL LESSON PLAN - LEARNING STYLES

ACTIVITIES - STUDENT CHOICES

Concrete Sequential

1. Make a time line showing famous inventions.

2. Develop a chart comparing and contrasting the telephone, computer & television.

3. Draw a diagram of your invention for improving transportation to and from school.

Abstract Sequential

4. Read a biography about a famous inventor. Give an oral report to the class.

5. Write and illustrate a booklet showing how an invention works.

6. Make your list of the ten most important inventions of the 21st century. Give reasons why these are the most important.

Concrete Random

7. Cut out a full-sized person from butcher paper. Make him a famous inventor. Write about him in the cut-out.

8. Construct a model of a new invention. Explain how it works.

9. Working in a small group, list 20 objects. Put them in random pairs. Then brainstorm all the possible inventions.

Abstract Random

10. Choose an important invention. Debate its merits with a classmate.

11. Develop a group skit showing what would have happened if video games had not been invented.

12. Read about several inventors. Identify common characteristics and report to your class.

Required Activities
Teacher's Choice

1. Read chapter on inventions in text. Outline or make a web of the information.

2. Define vocabulary words about inventions.

3. Listen to talk by guest speaker, a local inventor. Write a summary of what he/she said.

Product/Performance
Required

1. Outline or web

2. Definitions

3. Summary

Assessment
Required Activities

1. Understanding of main ideas and details; entire chapter included

2. Accuracy, complete

3. Main points included. Correct spelling, punctuation and grammar

Optional
Student-Parent
Cooperative Activity

Student Choices in
Ways to Learn

Concrete Sequential
_____

Concrete Random
_____

Abstract Sequential
_____

Abstract Random
_____

Product/Performance
Student Choice

Standards

Due Date
Student Choice

INDIVIDUAL LESSON PLAN - LEARNING STYLES

Required Activities Teacher's Choice	Product/Performance Required	Assessment Required Activities

Optional Student-Parent Cooperative Activity		Standards

Student Choices in Ways to Learn	Product/Performance Student Choice	Due Date Student Choice
Concrete Sequential _____ Concrete Random _____ Abstract Sequential _____ Abstract Random _____		

ACTIVITIES - STUDENT CHOICES

Concrete Sequential	Concrete Random

Abstract Sequential	Abstract Random

Structuring Student Choices

When giving students choices based on learning style, it is important for them to experience working in more than one learning style. Everyone has a learning style preference; however in adult life we have to learn to function in all four. I have an Abstract Random learning style preference, yet I function in the Concrete Sequential style when I am catching a plane or scheduling workshops! No one has the luxury of remaining in just one style. For this reason, structure Student Choices so that each student has to work in at least two different styles. For example, you might have each student choose two activities from one style and one from a different style.

It is up to each teacher to decide how to structure the choices.

Remember, when you use the **Individual Lesson Plan**™ (ILP) format you need to have some type of a timetable or schedule so that both the student and the teacher will know the due date for products and assignments. The best way to do this is to establish due dates when you review each of the Student Choice activities with the groups of students who have chosen the same activities. Have students write due dates in the block on the lower right-hand corner of the **ILP**™.

Using the Individual Lesson Plan Format™
in the Mixed Ability Classroom

In a mixed ability classroom you can use these activities for everyone. Design easier choices and more difficult choices. If you want all students to have the same choices, differentiate the quality, level, and expectations for the products for gifted and other high-ability students. Do this by embedding extensions of the activities in the assessments. See Chapter 7 for more information on ways to do this.

Students can also think of their own activities and write them on the **ILP**™ in the appropriate places. These self-generated choices give you even greater flexibility to individualize for your students. Encourage your gifted students to think of specific higher-level thinking activities they would like to do and write them on the **ILP**™. This also gives you an opportunity to help lower ability students choose activities that are not as difficult as the general Student Choice activities.

Another option is to encourage higher-level thinking by using **Questivities**™ along with the Student Choice activities. See pages 118 - 119 for more information.

Reflections

* Learning styles indicate the ways in which people process information.

* Dr. Anthony Gregorc has identified four basic learning styles:

- concrete sequential

- abstract sequential

- concrete random

- abstract random

* Students need to learn how to identify their strong and weak styles and become adept at working in all styles.

* Use the **Individual Lesson Plan™ (ILP)** format to plan student activities appropriate for each learning style.

Notes_____

"Our chief need in life is someone who will make us do what we can."
Ralph Waldo Emerson

Chapter 3

Learning Modalities

Questions to Consider

1. What do learning modalities indicate?

2. What are the four learning modalities?

3. How can learning modalities be included when planning curriculum, units, and lessons?

4. How can Student Choices be structured?

Children learn in very different ways. A number of theories help educators understand these many differences in students. Some reflect individual differences in abilities or experiences, but educators can categorize and work with other differences by examining learning modalities. Like the learning styles discussed in the last chapter, the learning modalities that students use are another way to look at student learning.

The theory of learning modalities was initially developed in the 1970s by Walter Barbe and Raymond Swassing. It was originally used in Special Education. If a student could not learn using one modality, perhaps we could teach him/her the same information using a different modality. For example, a blind person cannot learn to read using the visual modality, but he can learn braille which uses the kinesthetic modality to teach reading.

Learning modalities indicate the modes, or means through which people acquire information and the means by which they show what they know. Traditionally, educators have worked with three of these: Visual, Auditory, and Kinesthetic. I have changed Auditory to Verbal, reflecting both oral and written expression. In the 21st century Information Age, we need to add a fourth modality: Technological. While technology incorporates elements of the other three, the mental processes, specific tools, and pieces of equipment students use when dealing with technology are significantly different from the other three to warrant a fourth category.

While most students learn to gather and work with information in all four ways, each student usually has a modality strength. Identify their preferred modalities by observing your students, It is not necessary for students to always acquire information in their preferred mode, but make an effort to allow them to choose their modality when possible. Motivating students is easier when they can do a task using the modality they prefer.

Because modalities show both how we acquire information and how we show what we know, students often use at least two modalities while doing one learning activity. For example, a student working on a collage is taking in information using the kinesthetic modality as he cuts and pastes pictures onto a posterboard. The finished product, however, is visual, and he shows what he knows using the visual modality.

Besides having strengths in one modality, some students may also have specific weaknesses in a particular modality. Often this is the case with students identified with learning disabilities, attention deficit disorder, or other learning difficulties or problems. By identifying areas of strength and weakness, you can more readily individualize the learning activities to best meet the requirements of students with special needs.

Gifted/ high-ability learners often have tremendous strengths in one modality but are weaker in the others. Contrary to popular opinion, gifted students are not usually gifted in every learning area or every modality. The gifted may resist activities in which they will not excel, though it is appropriate to challenge them by having them complete activities that do not come easily.

The Visual Modality

Benita is a good reader. She can recognize more words by sight than almost anyone else in her second grade class. When she is in the car or at the grocery store with her mom, she reads the road signs and food labels. Benita loves to draw and can usually visualize the finished product before she begins working on it. When her dad takes her to the playground on Saturdays, she calls out to him repeatedly, "Look at me! Look at me!" Playing isn't very much fun for her unless someone is watching what she is doing. When she wants to rearrange her room, she draws her plan on a piece of paper before moving the furniture around. Benita's learning modality is visual.

Students with *strengths* in the visual modality:

- learn by seeing, watching demonstrations

- can recall the placement of words and pictures on a page

- are good with detail

- like descriptive reading

- learn from visual display and color

- recognize words by sight and people by face rather than name

- remember what they have written down because they can picture it

- have a vivid imagination and think in pictures

- are deliberate problem solvers and plan solutions and answers before acting and responding

- use facial expressions that are a good indication of their emotions

- take in many visual images but may not concentrate on one image for a long period of time

Favorite Phrases

"Do you see what I mean?"
"Look at me!"
"Look at my work."

Students with *weaknesses* in the visual modality:

- often turn in papers that are not neatly done

- read numbers, mathematical signs, or directions incorrectly

- do not do well on map activities

- get words or letters backwards

- leave out letters or words when writing

- don't notice when a room is redecorated

- have trouble copying from the board

- don't like to play Scrabble® or do crossword puzzles

Visual Products and Activities

Products

- ❑ charts
- ❑ illustrations
- ❑ filmstrips
- ❑ films
- ❑ graphs
- ❑ collages
- ❑ murals
- ❑ maps
- ❑ time lines
- ❑ flow charts
- ❑ diagrams
- ❑ posters

Activities

- ❑ observe
- ❑ copy
- ❑ illustrate
- ❑ design
- ❑ imagine
- ❑ color
- ❑ draw
- ❑ read

Additional Products and Activities:

The Verbal (Written & Auditory) Modality

Laurel loves to talk. She talks a lot with her friends, but she also talks to herself when she is trying to learn something, repeating the information over and over. Her favorite assignment in school this year was writing a poem about the environment. Her poem had so many 'plays on words' everyone thought it was hilarious. All of the lines rhymed, too. Laurel keeps a journal where she writes out all of her problems. She then talks about these problems with her mom and her best friend. She usually explains the problem to them and then asks, "Do you hear what I'm saying?" Laurel is a verbal learner.

Students with *strengths* in the verbal modality:

- learn through verbal instructions from others or themselves

- like oral language

- enjoy dialogues, skits, and debates

- have auditory word attack skills and learn words phonetically

- talk to themselves and repeat information verbally, especially when memorizing

- are distracted by sounds

- talk out problems and the pros and cons of a situation, and try out solutions verbally

- express emotion through changes in pitch, tone and volume of voice

- enjoy listening but are always ready to talk

- like music, rap, poetry, rhyming words

- are not detail people; tend to be global thinkers

- learn through verbal repetition

Favorite Phrases

"Do you hear what I'm saying?"

"I'm just thinking out loud."

Students with *weaknesses* in the verbal modality:

- find it easier to show or demonstrate something than to tell about it

- know what they want to say but have a hard time finding the right words

- ask others to repeat what they've just said

- have difficulty listening in class

Verbal Products and Activities

Products

- ❏ oral reports
- ❏ role plays
- ❏ simulations
- ❏ panel discussions
- ❏ debates
- ❏ lectures
- ❏ skits
- ❏ poetry
- ❏ songs
- ❏ audio tapes
- ❏ short stories

Activities

- ❏ interview
- ❏ discuss
- ❏ talk about
- ❏ recite
- ❏ debate
- ❏ share
- ❏ respond
- ❏ explain
- ❏ list
- ❏ brainstorm
- ❏ paraphrase
- ❏ sing
- ❏ memorize
- ❏ read
- ❏ write

Additional Products and Activities:

The Kinesthetic Modality

Allen is a hands-on person. He loves to build models and has a big display of model airplanes and model cars in his room. He also enjoys watching adventure movies and likes to play basketball with his friends. In school his favorite subject is science because his teacher lets the students do lots of real experiments. Last week he actually was able to dissect a frog! Sometimes he gets in trouble at school because he wiggles around and is always out of his seat. He went to the principal's office a couple of times for fighting. Allen thinks school would be better if the teachers gave more assignments that dealt with 'real life'. When Allen finishes talking to someone on the phone he often says, "I'll be in touch with you again later." He functions best using the kinesthetic learning modality.

Students with *strengths* in the kinesthetic modality*:*

- learn by direct involvement and hands-on experiences

- prefer action/adventure stories and videos

- remember what they have done more readily than what they have seen or read

- experiment with ideas to see how they will work in the real world

- touch, feel, manipulate, and play with objects

- show emotions physically by jumping, hugging, applauding, etc.

- communicate feelings through body language

- enjoy the performing arts and athletics

- like working with materials, machinery, and tools

> **Favorite Phrases**
> *"How does that grab you?"*
> *"Are you in touch with that?"*

Students with *weaknesses* in the kinesthetic modality:

- are not good at sports

- may be seen as clumsy and awkward

- are unskilled in working with their hands

- have trouble putting puzzles together

- would rather be a spectator than a participant

- may say they have "two left feet"

Kinesthetic Products and Activities

Products
- ❏ dioramas
- ❏ puzzles
- ❏ games
- ❏ sculptures
- ❏ models
- ❏ puppets
- ❏ scrapbooks
- ❏ murals
- ❏ skits
- ❏ pantomimes
- ❏ mobiles

Activities
- ❏ assemble
- ❏ construct
- ❏ invent
- ❏ sort
- ❏ put together
- ❏ build
- ❏ design
- ❏ experiment
- ❏ manipulate

<u>*Additional Products and Activities:*</u>

The Technological Modality

From the time he was in first grade, Mark was the one teachers would call on to figure out any problem they were having with the computer. Even at a very young age, Mark seemed to have a natural affinity for technology. As computers became more powerful, Mark began writing his own programs, developing databases, designing computerized graphic images, and learning to integrate audio and video into his school reports. Mark does much better work when he uses technological tools to accomplish assignments. His reports done on the word processor and complex math problems solved with the aid of a calculator are superior to the work he does without technological aids. Mark has many online friends from all over the world with whom he corresponds regularly via e-mail. Mark learns best through the technological learning modality.

Students with *strengths* in the technological modality

- would like to learn everything technologically

- enjoy using a digital camera

- are mechanically oriented

- finds every possible use for any new technological gadget

- like integrated technologies and learning activities

- have highly-developed Internet research skills

- interact and communicate with others via e-mail, instant messaging and/or the Internet

- know how to work with and use new software programs and new hardware without reading the directions

- spend much of their spare time on the computer or playing video games have better quality work and thinking when using technological tools

Favorite Phrases

"Would you give me your input on that?"

"I'm on overload!"

Students with *weaknesses* in the technological modality:

- spend as little time as possible on the computer

- get frustrated with technology when it doesn't work right and don't have strategies that might fix it

- don't like to experiment with new ways to do things technologically

- would rather write something by hand instead of using the word processor

- will let their partner do all of the hands-on work at the computer while they just sit and watch

Technological Products and Activities

Products

- ❑ computer-generated reports with graphics
- ❑ slide shows from digital camera
- ❑ PowerPoint and multimedia presentations
- ❑ TV or radio shows
- ❑ reviews & evaluations of web sites
- ❑ word processing documents

Activities

- ❑ using software packages for individualized learning
- ❑ using interactive whiteboards
- ❑ taking online courses
- ❑ making and editing videos
- ❑ participating in interactive video conferencing
- ❑ doing an e-mail interview

Additional Products and Activities:

Learning Modalities

Teacher Reflection Page

1. List the names of one or more of your students for each modality. Give examples of how they have used this modality to acquire and work with information.

Visual:

Verbal:

Kinesthetic:

Technological:

2. Which modality are you most comfortable using?

Describe ways you have used this modality in your own learning.

3. Which modality is least comfortable for you? Why?

Learning Modalities

Classroom Activities

Which modalities do you incorporate in your classroom?

1. List several activities you typically use with students in your classroom. Indicate the modality each is most suited for.

Classroom activity

Learning modality:
_____

Classroom activity

Learning modality:
_____

Classroom activity

Learning modality:
_____

2. What teaching activities or materials that you have not been using could you use to facilitate learning in each modality?

Visual:

Verbal:

Kinesthetic:

Technological:

Using the Individual Lesson Plan™ (ILP) Format to Plan Units Incorporating Learning Modalities

Use the Planner on page 18 to generate ideas for unit activities. After you have done the initial planning of your unit, decide which activities you want all of your students to do. List these activities in the block in the center of the **Individual Lesson Plan™ (ILP)** format which is labeled Required Activities - Teacher's Choice. List the resulting products/performances and assessment criteria in the two blocks on the right.

Now look at the remainder of the activities. Examine how students will gather information as they do each activity. If you have not listed very many activities in a particular modality, you can often make a small change so that the activity will fit a different modality than you had originally planned. These activities become the Student Choice Activities. Review the characteristics for each learning modality. Decide which activities would be appropriate for each.

In planning the *Inventors and Inventions* unit, one activity chosen for the visual learner is to make a collage of 19th and 20th century inventions. This activity works well for a visual learner who likes visual display and color and who thinks in pictures. An activity appropriate for the verbal learner is debating who the most important inventor of the 20th century is, because this is the type of student who likes dialogue, skits, and debates. For the kinesthetic student, one appropriate activity is to invent a 3-dimensional game about inventors. Remember this student likes to touch, feel, and manipulate objects. Finally, for the technological learner, one activity is to learn about an invention by looking at web sites, because this type of learner likes learning everything via the computer.

On the next page is the **Individual Lesson Plan™ (ILP)** with the Student Choices focusing on Learning Modalities. A reproducible blank format with Student Choices by learning modalities is on the following page. Use this to design your own units.

Structuring Student Choices

Since students need to learn to work with information through all four modes, structure the Student Choices so that they must make choices in at least two different modalities. Students write their choices directly on the **Individual Lesson Plan™ (ILP)**, as in the Learning Styles **ILP™**.

Most students are anxious to try technological learning. However, your choices in this area may depend on the availability of technological equipment in your classroom or school. If this is a problem, brainstorm ways to get more equipment with your students, your parents, and/or your administration.

INDIVIDUAL LESSON PLAN - LEARNING MODALITIES

ACTIVITIES - STUDENT CHOICES

Visual

1. Make a Venn Diagram comparing/contrasting copyrights & patents. Write a paragraph about which one you think is most important & why.

2. Make a crossword puzzle of Leonardo DaVinci's inventions.

3. Make a collage of 19th century or 20th century inventions.

Kinesthetic

4. Create a best friend robot and list 10 things you would like it to do.

5. Make an invention from paper and explain how it works.

6. Invent a game about inventors. Include a 3-D gameboard.

Verbal

7. Debate with a classmate: The most important invention of the 20th century is . . . because . . .

8. Using appropriate visual aids do an oral report about the car. Include your car of the future.

9. Write your list of the ten most important inventions. Persuade the class that your list is correct.

Technological

10. Produce a 2 minute musical video selling yourself as a robot.

11. Survey 25 people with home computers to find out what kind they have. Generate a graph showing survey results.

12. Locate three websites that give information about an invention. Write a short paper evaluating them.

Required Activities
Teacher's Choice

1. Read text about inventions & inventors. Answer text questions.
2. View video about major inventions of the 20th century. Make a concept map of important inventions.
3. Write a news story about one important inventor.

Optional Student-Parent Cooperative Activity

Student Choices in Ways to Learn

Visual

_____

Kinesthetic

_____

Verbal

_____

Technological

_____

Product/Performance Required

1. Answers to questions

2. Concept map

3. News story

Product/Performance Student Choice

Assessment
Required Activities

1. Accurate; complete

2. Main ideas recorded; appropriate details & facts

3. Organization; clarity of thought, accurate information

Standards

Due Date
Student Choice

INDIVIDUAL LESSON PLAN - LEARNING MODALITIES

Assessment
Required Activities

Product/Performance
Required

Required Activities
Teacher's Choice

Standards

Optional
Student-Parent
Cooperative Activity

Due Date
Student Choice

Product/Performance
Student Choice

Student Choices in
Ways to Learn

Visual _____

Kinesthetic _____

Verbal _____

Technological _____

ACTIVITIES - STUDENT CHOICES

Verbal

Technological

Visual

Kinesthetic

Reflections

* Learning modalities indicate the modes or means through which people acquire and work with information and ways they show what they know.

* The four learning modalities discussed in this chapter are

- Visual

- Verbal

- Kinesthetic

- Technological

* In planning curriculum, thematic units, and lessons teachers need to include activities and products appropriate for each modality.

* We can structure student choices so that students can make limited vs unlimited choices. Base the choices on your situation, needs, and standards.

Notes

Chapter 4

Bloom's Taxonomy of Educational Objectives

Questions to Consider

1. What will help me structure leveled objectives, learning activities, and educational outcomes for my students?

2. What are the levels of Bloom's Taxonomy?

3. How can I use the Individual Lesson Plan™ (ILP) format with Bloom's Taxonomy?

4. How can using Bloom's Taxonomy help me to differentiate the curriculum?

Taxonomies are **classification schemes developed to delineate educational goals, objectives, and outcomes**. They provide a way for us to understand and develop questions, and because they are descriptions of types of behavior, they are observable.

When I was an undergraduate in the College of Education, one of the first educational ideas I learned was Bloom's Taxonomy. It has been part of my educational philosophy ever since then. I believe it continues to be a powerful tool for educators. It is extremely useful in providing guidance and structure as teachers plan objectives, leveled learning activities, and educational outcomes for their students.

Bloom's Taxonomy, also called the Taxonomy of Educational Objectives, is a frequently used model for developing higher-level thinking skills. It is a process-oriented model that allows teachers to present ideas and concepts at many different levels. In this way, teachers can use it to tier activities, thereby differentiating their instruction to meet the needs of a variety of learners.

It is important to stimulate the brain at all levels; therefore, expose all students to learning activities and experiences at different levels of the Taxonomy. Often teachers choose simple objectives that require little student thinking. These tend to be at the lower levels of the Taxonomy. When this happens, it is a cause for concern because we need to optimize the learning potential of all our students.

We often think of Bloom's Taxonomy as a linear model, but we can also view it as cyclical, with the evaluation level creating new information to be learned at the Knowledge level. It can also be seen as a structure that facilitates a free flow of ideas and activities between the different levels. Teachers must be able to assess how much each student knows and comprehends about a given topic of study to know how much time each student needs to spend working at the lower levels of the Taxonomy. Some students bring a large amount of knowledge to class with them and are ready to move to the higher levels very quickly.

The Taxonomy may be new to you. On the other hand, you may have learned about Bloom's Taxonomy years ago. You may have used it from time to time in planning lessons and activities or in examining performance levels for your students. Continue to use it or become reacquainted with it. This Taxonomy of Educational Objectives is an important tool for 21st century teachers.

The Six Levels of Bloom's Taxonomy

Knowledge - Acquiring/learning facts

Comprehension - Understanding the information on a basic level

Application - Using the information in a new context

Analysis - Examining the information in detail, one part at a time

Synthesis - Understanding the information in relation to the whole

Evaluation - Assessing the information based on agreed-upon criteria

Level 1 - Knowledge

Ability to:

- bring to mind appropriate material and answers

- recall or recognize specific information

This level addresses the knowledge of specific facts and terminology, the ways students can deal with these specific facts, and categories or patterns of knowledge.

For example, in *Inventors & Inventions* at the knowledge level a student makes a poster of any three inventors and their inventions.

Representative Activities		**Representative Products**
Define	Describe	List
Label	Locate	Definition
Recite	Select	Outline
Memorize	Recognize	Map location
Name	State	Answers to reproductive question
Identify	Repeat	
Tell		
List		

Level 2 - Comprehension

Ability to:

- understand the information given or communicated

- make use of an idea in the same or similar situation

This level addresses the ways students interpret information.

For example, in *Inventors & Inventions* a student explains how the invention of his choice works.

Representative Activities

Restate	Paraphrase
Rewrite	Convert
Give examples	Illustrate
Summarize	Explain
Locate	Express
Translate	Edit

Representative Products

Essay	Diagram
Oral report	Drawing
Mural	Map with location noted
Revision	Translation
Illustration	

Level 3 - Application

Ability to:

- use ideas, theories, methods, concepts, or principles in new situations

- use something in a different way

This level addresses the use of abstractions in particular situations.

For example, in *Inventors & Inventions* if a student has knowledge of which inventions have helped senior citizens lead safer lives, she could make a collection of these inventions and explain to a group of senior citizens how to use them.

Representative Activities

Apply	Modify
Dramatize	Cook
Demonstrate	Construct
Build	Make

Representative Products

Puzzle	Collection
Diorama	Model
Mobile	Demonstration
Diary	Journal

Level 4 - Analysis

Ability to:

- break down into smaller parts

- make something clearer by examining it closely

This level addresses the breaking of the whole into parts to distinguish elements, relationships, or organizational principles.

For example, in *Inventors & Inventions* a student could develop a chart to compare and contrast similarities and differences among several different types of aircraft.

Representative Activities

Analyze	Classify
Distinguish	Subdivide
Separate	Differentiate
Examine	Calculate
Categorize	Investigate
Compare/contrast	

Representative Products

Graph
Questionnaire
Survey
Chart
List of parts or classifications
Venn diagram

Level 5 - Synthesis

Ability to:

- put together parts into a unified whole

- express original thoughts or make original products

This level addresses putting parts together in a new form such as in a new piece of writing or other form of communication, a new plan, or a new invention.

For example, in *Inventors & Inventions* a student might develop a new invention that combines both music and math.

Representative Activities

Combine	Compose
Design	Organize
Invent	Develop
Plan	Create
Imagine	Forecast

Representative Products

Invention	News article
Story	Poem
Play/skit	Original game
Plan of action	Advertisement

Level 6 - Evaluation

Ability to:

- judge the value of something according to specified criteria

- develop and apply standards and criteria

This level addresses making judgments based on logical evidence, external facts, and/or established criteria.

For example, in *Inventors & Inventions* a student could decide on criteria for judging the best form of transportation for the 21st century.

Representative Activities

Judge
Recommend
Debate
Give opinion
Rate

Evaluate
Summarize
Criticize
Prioritize

Representative Products

Critique
Portfolio
Summary of group discussion
Review of a play, book, song, etc.
Evaluation form with criteria listed
Editorial
Position paper
Pro and con chart with conclusions

"A civilized society is one in which people have an appreciation of and a concern with the incredibly wide range of human needs, capacities and potentialities."

Dr. Alice Tay, Professor, University of Sydney

Assessing Thinking Skills
Using Bloom's Taxonomy

When forming objectives and outcomes for your students, learn to assess which levels of the Taxonomy they use. This assessment form will help you analyze your learning activities by showing you in which levels of the Taxonomy your students will be working when they do a particular activity. Check all that apply.

Name of Activity _____

1. Knowledge

❑ Ability to recall or recognize specific information
❑ Ability to bring to mind appropriate answers

2. Comprehension

❑ Ability to understand what is being communicated
❑ Ability to make use of an idea in the same or similar situation

3. Application

❑ Ability to use ideas in new situations
❑ Ability to use something in a different way

4. Analysis

❑ Ability to break down into smaller parts
❑ Ability to make something clearer by examining it closely

5. Synthesis

❑ Ability to put together parts into a unified whole
❑ Ability to express original thoughts or make original products

6. Evaluation

❑ Ability to develop standards and criteria
❑ Ability to judge the value of something according to specified criteria

Structuring Student Choices Using the ILP™ Format

As with Learning Styles and Learning Modalities in the previous two chapters, one way to ensure exposure to all students of the various levels of the Taxonomy is to use the **Individual Lesson Plan™ (ILP)** format. In this case, Bloom's Taxonomy will provide the structure for the Student Choice learning activities.

When using Bloom's Taxonomy with the **Individual Lesson Plan™ (ILP)** format, require that all students choose at least one or two items from the four higher levels of the Taxonomy (application, analysis, synthesis and evaluation). This will ensure that every student is engaged in activities requiring higher-level thinking skills. Some students need to do very little at the lower levels of the Taxonomy because they already have the knowledge and comprehension about a given topic. Other students may not have the background knowledge and therefore would need to do more at this level. You can structure individual choices so as to meet the learning needs of each of your students.

The sample **Individual Lesson Plans™ (ILPs)** on pages 63 and 65 show two approaches to Bloom's Taxonomy. The **ILP**™ on page 63 has all six levels included in the Student Choice activities. The **ILP**™ on page 65 has only the four higher levels in the Student Choice activities. In this case, the Knowledge and Comprehension levels are included in the Teacher Required activities. Two blank **Individual Lesson Plan™ (ILP)** formats structured for Bloom's Taxonomy can be found on pages 64 and 66. Use the blank formats to create your own units of study.

Reflections

* Bloom's Taxonomy provides a structure for planning objectives, learning activities, and educational outcomes for students.

* There are six levels of Bloom's Taxonomy: knowledge, comprehension, application, analysis, synthesis, and evaluation.

* Students can be exposed to learning activities in all levels of the Taxonomy by using the Individual Lesson Plan™ (ILP) format.

* Bloom's Taxonomy is useful in planning tiered lessons and ILPs™ with different levels for different students.

INDIVIDUAL LESSON PLAN - BLOOM'S TAXONOMY

ACTIVITIES - STUDENT CHOICES

Knowledge

1. Make a poster of any three inventors and their inventions.

2. E-mail Disney World's Epcot Center to get information about inventions of tomorrow. Write a report about them.

Comprehension

3. Write a mini-book explaining how the invention of your choice works.

4. Draw a cartoon that features an invention of the future and shows its functions.

Application

5. Make a chart of safety inventions for senior citizens. Share with groups of seniors.

6. Role play a typical day before electricity was invented.

Analysis

7. Develop a chart comparing and contrasting several different types of aircraft.

8. Present an oral report discussing problems in transition from the Industrial Age to the Information Age.

Synthesis

9. Brainstorm all the functions you would like your personal robot to have. Then make a diagram of your robot showing how it would work.

10. Invent a new product that combines music and math.

Evaluation

11. Write a letter to Thomas Edison explaining why one of his inventions is so important.

12. Decide on criteria for judging the best form of transportation for the 21st Century. Make a chart evaluating 3 types of transportation using your criteria.

Required Activities
Teacher's Choice

1. Read chapter in text that highlights significant inventions. Outline major ideas and details.

2. View video about important inventors of the 19th and 20th centuries. Write a summary.

3. Visit a local museum that features inventions from your state. Draw a diagram of one invention there.

Product/Performance Required

1. Outline

2. Summary

3. Diagram

Assessment
Required Activities

1. Choice of ideas and facts; accuracy

2. Clarity of thought; important details included

3. Appropriate visual; accuracy of information

Optional Student-Parent Cooperative Activity

Student Choices in Ways to Learn

Knowledge

Comprehension

Application

Analysis

Synthesis

Evaluation

Product/Performance Student Choice

Standards

Due Date Student Choice

©2005 Carolyn Coil and Pieces of Learning

INDIVIDUAL LESSON PLAN - BLOOM'S TAXONOMY

ACTIVITIES - STUDENT CHOICES

Assessment Required Activities	Product/Performance Required	Required Activities Teacher's Choice

Standards

Optional Student-Parent Cooperative Activity

Due Date Student Choice	Product/Performance Student Choice	Student Choices in Ways to Learn
		Knowledge _____ Comprehension _____ Application _____ Analysis _____ Synthesis _____ Evaluation _____

Analysis	Synthesis	Evaluation

Knowledge	Comprehension	Application

©2005 Carolyn Coil and Pieces of Learning

INDIVIDUAL LESSON PLAN - BLOOM'S TAXONOMY - HIGHER LEVELS

ACTIVITIES - STUDENT CHOICES

Application	Synthesis
1. Make a model of an invention that would do your homework automatically. 2. List twenty inventions in your house that you or your family use on a daily basis. For each item, list how you would do the invention's functions if you didn't have the invention.	5. Design a house that stays cool in the summer and warm in the winter through an alternate energy source. 6. Write a short story that shows changes in life due to inventions that have been invented since 1950.

Analysis	Evaluation
3. Make a diagram of any invention. Write an explanation of the functions of each part and how they interact with one another in order for the invention to work properly. 4. Make a list of five inventions that have harmed the environment. For each invention, analyze the types of harm and for each invention, suggest one way the environment could be improved.	7. Which invention that you or your family now use could you most easily live without? Write a position paper with five reasons to defend and show how you would live without it. 8. Choose an important inventor. Research his or her life and identify three things that happened that made him or her a good inventor. Give reasons for your answers.

Required Activities
Teacher's Choice

1. Read background information about how inventions affect everyday life. Take notes as you read.

2. Make a time line of the ten most important inventions in your life. Include the date invented, the name of the inventor, and other important facts.

Optional
Student-Parent
Cooperative Activity

Student Choices in
Ways to Learn

Application _____

Analysis _____

Synthesis _____

Evaluation _____

Product/Assessment Required

1. Notes from reading

2. Time line

Product/Performance
Student Choice

Assessment
Required Activities

1. Complete for reading done; accurate; readable

2. Follow Rubric page 107

Standards

Due Date
Student Choice

©2005 Carolyn Coil and Pieces of Learning

INDIVIDUAL LESSON PLAN - BLOOM'S TAXONOMY - HIGHER LEVELS

Assessment
Required Activities

Product/Assessment
Required

Required Activities
Teacher's Choice

Standards

Due Date
Student Choice

Product/Performance
Student Choice

Optional
Student-Parent
Cooperative Activity

Student Choices in
Ways to Learn

Application _____

Analysis _____

Synthesis _____

Evaluation _____

ACTIVITIES - STUDENT CHOICES

Synthesis

Evaluation

Applicaton

Analysis

©2005 Carolyn Coil and Pieces of Learning

Chapter 5

Multiple Intelligences

Questions to Consider

1. What is intelligence?

2. Which intelligences are identified by Gardner's Theory of Multiple Intelligences?

3. Can intelligence be developed and taught?

4. Do all students have multiple intelligences?

Mr. Briggs looked at Robyn, one of his most outstanding students. "She is so intelligent," he thought to himself. "She reads and writes beautifully and her work in math is always tops. I wish some of my other students were as intelligent as she is!"

In the above scenario, Mr. Briggs was describing the ways Robyn functioned in several tasks, activities, and challenges she faces in school. To him, her responses in these areas define what an intelligent student is. Mr. Briggs, however, has a narrow view of intelligence, for his view focuses on verbal and mathematical tasks. He is not alone. Many of us who work in education have generally defined intelligence in a similar way.

But intellectual differences among people are much broader than this. To understand the concept of intelligence more fully, we need to examine the Theory of Multiple Intelligences.

An Overview of Multiple Intelligences

Harvard University psychologist Howard Gardner developed his Theory of Multiple Intelligences in the early 1980s. Saying educators and other experts had defined intelligence too narrowly, he stated that intelligence involves several different ways of solving problems and creating products. He demonstrated that each individual has a unique intelligence profile that shows relative strengths and weaknesses in all of the Multiple Intelligences. Each intelligence, he says, is modifiable and is sparked and activated by a variety of stimuli. Generally speaking, because of differences in culture and experience, in individuals some intelligences develop as dominant intelligences, others moderately, and others slightly.

The Multiple Intelligences relate directly to whatever information or content is being considered. This means they are content based, rather than existing by themselves with no relationship to content. Handling different types of information leads to the development of different types of abilities. Intelligence is not a single fixed trait that can be assigned a single number for life! In fact, according to Gardner, we can develop and teach intelligence.

He came to this conclusion and developed his Theory of Multiple Intelligences after studying children at the Boston University School of Medicine, the Veterans Administration Medical Center in Boston, and at Harvard's Project Zero which sought to develop and enhance a variety of intelligences in young children.

Intelligence and culture are interdependent. Different cultures put value on different types of intelligence. As a middle class white American, I have a highly developed verbal intelligence. My culture values this type of intelligence. Recently, however, I had the privilege of visiting an Aboriginal community at Daly River in the Northern Territory of Australia. As we drove from Darwin to Daly River, I began to sense the vastness and the silence of the Australian outback. The terrain changed subtly and seemed to stretch forever. I soon realized that the visual/spatial and naturalist intelligences (my weak areas) would be much more valued in this environment than verbal ability. In this setting, I would not be considered very intelligent at all! This experience helped me understand the interrelatedness of one's culture and the development of one's intelligences.

The Multiple Intelligences function as a bridge between the learning modalities that indicate how one takes in information and shows what he knows and learning styles that reflect how an individual processes information inside the brain.

Multiple Intelligences reflect the intelligence we <u>use</u> as we process the information. For example, right now you are probably using your Verbal/Linguistic and your Intrapersonal intelligences as you process the information in this book.

Gardner suggests that each individual possesses at least eight different intelligences. Each person possesses a unique blend of these intelligences. In order to study and understand them, we can analyze each. But in "real life" people use them in combination with one another and not just one at a time.

Gardner believes that virtually everyone has the capacity to develop all of the Multiple Intelligences. The Intelligences usually work together and interact with one another in complex ways. Most of the time when solving a problem, creating a product, or interacting with the environment, people use more than one intelligence. A student preparing for a debate, for example, will use Verbal/Linguistic intelligence but also Mathematical/Logical and Interpersonal intelligence.

Each Intelligence exhibits itself in several ways. For example, both a very quiet person who writes an excellent descriptive paragraph and a talkative person who tells a beautiful story but cannot write very well exhibit Verbal/Linguistic intelligence. Dancers or athletes who are performing and a craftsperson who is working very carefully with his hands all exhibit Bodily/Kinesthetic intelligence. A mural with splashy brilliant colors and an architect's intricate drawings are both examples of Visual/Spatial intelligence.

The 3 Main Categories of
Gardner's Multiple Intelligences

I. Language related	II. Object related	III. Personal related
Verbal/Linguistic	Logical/Mathematical	Intrapersonal
Musical/Rhythmic	Visual/Spatial	Interpersonal
	Bodily/Kinesthetic	
	Naturalist	

I. Language Related Intelligences

Verbal/Linguistic   Musical/Rhythmic

Described as "object free" intelligences, these two intelligences are reflected in the variety and forms of languages written and spoken all over the earth.

Verbal/Linguistic Intelligence

The ability to use language for a variety of purposes including to persuade, inform, communicate, solve problems, aid in memorization, entertain, and acquire new knowledge

Jeremy, a first grader, knows he is the best reader in his class. He loves to read and began reading when he was three years old. His mom and dad read to him every night, and his dad always tells him a funny story before bedtime. His grandma gives him read-along books for every birthday, and he loves to listen to the stories as he turns the pages. He is learning to write sentences and paragraphs on a computer program at school. He is full of questions. Last week he wanted to know why the Smoky Mountains look like they are surrounded by smoke and why Kansas isn't near the ocean. He always has a new joke to tell his classmates and never forgets the punch line! Jeremy has a highly developed verbal/linguistic intelligence.

Characteristics

- includes skill in speaking, writing, listening, and reading
- entails spoken and written language and its uses
- relates to ability to learn new languages easily
- involves the capacity to use words effectively
- helps students produce and refine language in its many forms and formats
- enriched by a wealth of vocabulary
- embraces the ability to understand the function of language

Representative Products

- ❑ Poem
- ❑ Speech
- ❑ Story
- ❑ Skit or play
- ❑ Newspaper article
- ❑ Oral report
- ❑ Word game
- ❑ Reaction paper

Representative Activities

- ❑ Participating in a debate
- ❑ Writing a research paper
- ❑ Listening to a guest speaker
- ❑ Creating a new ending for a myth
- ❑ Acting in a dramatic reading
- ❑ Composing a story or poem

Representative Careers

- ❑ Journalist
- ❑ Talk show host
- ❑ Speech writer
- ❑ Secretary

© Carolyn Coil

Musical/Rhythmic Intelligence

The ability to communicate or understand emotions and ideas conveyed through music and the ability to compose and/or perform musically. Ideas, memories, factual information, emotions, moods, important historical or cultural events all can be incorporated into the musical/rhythmic intelligence

> *Music has always been important to Ramon. When he was a little boy, special songs that he would hear at family gatherings seemed to bring all of them together. The radio is always blaring in his car and the CD player is always on in his room. Ramon is in 11th grade and has been in the school band since 7th grade. He practices his French horn every day and was excited to learn he has made first chair in the All-County band. Ramon has trouble in many of his academic subjects but finds he can memorize information if he puts it to music in his head. He has a highly developed musical/rhythmic intelligence.*

Characteristics

- is a form of language without words

- resides mostly in the right brain

- involves sensitivity to sounds and a good sense of pitch

- is often highly emotional

- powerful in establishing and conveying mood

- involves the capacity to perceive, discriminate, transform, and express musical forms

- includes both the intuitive understanding of music (such as playing an instrument "by ear") and a more formal, technical understanding (such as comes from the study of music theory)

- embraces rhythm, beat, and harmony

- may assist in developing other intelligences

- enhances memorization, math skills, and spatial abilities

Representative Products
- ❏ Song
- ❏ Audio musical advertisement
- ❏ Poem or rap
- ❏ Musical composition
- ❏ Musical performance
- ❏ Musical video

Representative Activities
- ❏ Verbal recall in unison
- ❏ Singing songs tied to curriculum outcomes
- ❏ Choral reading
- ❏ Creating musical mnemonics
- ❏ Playing musical instruments

Representative Careers
- ❏ Composer
- ❏ Ad writer
- ❏ Singer
- ❏ Instrumentalist
- ❏ Band director
- ❏ Music teacher

II. Object Related Intelligences

Logical/Mathematical   **Visual/Spatial**
Bodily/Kinesthetic   **Naturalist**

These four intelligences function along with the objects an individual works with when solving a problem or making a product.

Logical/Mathematical Intelligence

The ability to recognize and explore patterns, categories, and relationships using objects or mathematical symbols in a logical, ordered, sequential way

> *Carla is a third grader. She enjoys math, science, and technology in school. She feels these subjects are much more logical than other subjects where the questions seem to have no right or wrong answers. Carla likes working with numbers. She likes number games and logic puzzles. Though she is considered 'smart' by her classmates, Carla has trouble making friends. When she plays a game, she knows all the rules and is dogmatic about sticking to them. The other students think she is 'bossy' because she does this so often. When she disagrees with others, she feels her view is totally right and theirs is totally wrong. She explains all the reasons she is correct without really listening to what anyone else is saying. Carla would not win any popularity contests in her class!*

Characteristics

- incorporates mathematical and scientific abilities

- oriented toward rules, rubrics, and regulations

- characterized by both abstraction and exploration

- enjoys collecting and classifying things

- uses reasoning and logic to solve problems

- includes the capacity to use numbers effectively

- involves a sensitivity to logical patterns, statements, and relationships

- can be very abstract

- entails knowing the practicalities of how things work

Representative Products
- ❑ Graph
- ❑ Chart
- ❑ Time line
- ❑ Logic puzzle
- ❑ Venn diagram
- ❑ Solutions to math problems

Representative Activities
- ❑ Comparing/contrasting
- ❑ Outlining
- ❑ Categorizing
- ❑ Finding patterns
- ❑ Observing/collecting data

Representative Careers
- ❑ Engineer
- ❑ Statistician
- ❑ Computer programmer
- ❑ Scientist
- ❑ Accountant
- ❑ Web master
- ❑ Environmental regulator

Visual/Spatial Intelligence

The ability to perceive, create, and change visual objects mentally; create and interpret visual arts; orient oneself using maps, blueprints, or other visuals; navigate within an environment, specific space, or location

When 12- year-old Jennifer walks into a room, she immediately wants to redecorate it! She can picture the way it would look with a new color of paint, new wallpaper, and new carpet on the floor. Jennifer wears clothes with colors and patterns most people would not think to put together, but she has an 'eye' for creating new visual images that work. Jennifer's friends say she is very creative and artistic. She loves to draw and spends much time sketching and doodling, even when she should be doing something else. Her favorite class is art, and she loves doing projects in other classes where she can use her artistic abilities. Jennifer hopes to be an architect, clothing designer, or interior decorator when she grows up.

Characteristics

- involves ability to represent spatial information graphically

- uses ability to respond to and recreate the visual world & to see things in a way others would not

- includes sensitivity to color, line, shape, form, space, and the relationships that exist between these elements

- incorporates the capacity to both visualize and to physically orient oneself spatially

- entails understanding of the relationship of parts to the whole object

- related to ability to read and interpret maps, charts, and graphs

- requires a keen eye for visual detail

Representative Products

- ❏ Painting
- ❏ Model
- ❏ Collage
- ❏ Mural
- ❏ Map
- ❏ Cartoon/comic strip
- ❏ Video
- ❏ Photo
- ❏ Drawing
- ❏ Origami
- ❏ Chart/graph
- ❏ Web/mind map
- ❏ Computer graphic
- ❏ Diorama

Representative Activities

- ❏ Using visual/graphic organizers
- ❏ Making bulletin boards, posters, mobiles
- ❏ Learning through color coding, colorful overheads, slides, and videos
- ❏ Working with computer graphics programs
- ❏ Observing something and representing it visually

Representative Careers

- ❏ Cartographer
- ❏ Artist
- ❏ Photographer
- ❏ Graphic designer
- ❏ Clothing designer
- ❏ Food stylist
- ❏ Interior decorator
- ❏ Display artist

Bodily/Kinesthetic Intelligence

The ability to use both mind and body in the display of motor skills and the performance of physical tasks and to easily manipulate objects within one's environment

Tony is a ninth grader who is already considered a top player on the high school football team. He has always loved sports and has played football ever since he can remember. Tony keeps his body in good shape, working out at least two hours a day during the off season. Catching a pass, running with the ball, and eluding the other team's players comes as second nature to him. When he's not on the field, he often sees the game in his mind and mentally runs through the plays. Tony struggles academically and sometimes wishes reading, writing, and math would come as easy for him as playing football does.

Characteristics

- requires the use of both mind and body in thinking out actions before doing them

- involves expertise in using one's whole body to express ideas and feelings

- related to a good sense of balance and grace in movement

- entails solving problems by "doing"

- requires good eye-hand coordination

- includes ability to use one's hands to produce or transform things

- uses physical skills such as coordination, balance, strength, speed, and dexterity

- incorporates control of bodily motions and the ability to skillfully manipulate and interact with objects

Representative Products

- ❑ Sports performance
- ❑ Dance
- ❑ Item made by hand
- ❑ Skit/pantomime
- ❑ Oral presentation
- ❑ Carving/sculpture
- ❑ Poster
- ❑ 3 dimensional game
- ❑ Design
- ❑ Model
- ❑ Demonstration
- ❑ Construction

Representative Activities

- ❑ Role playing
- ❑ Creative movement
- ❑ Outdoor education
- ❑ Math
- ❑ Creating/inventing something
- ❑ Simulation
- ❑ Lab experiment
- ❑ Constructing model
- ❑ Cooperative learning
- ❑ Field trip
- ❑ Learning center
- ❑ Active learning

Representative Careers

- ❑ Sports medicine
- ❑ Chiropractor
- ❑ Building contractor
- ❑ Lab technician
- ❑ Dental hygienist
- ❑ Plumber
- ❑ Massage therapist
- ❑ Carpenter
- ❑ Repair person

Naturalist Intelligence

The ability to discern, identify, organize, and classify plants and animals; includes a keen sense of observation and the ability to seek, obtain, and put order to information about the natural world. These skills can be extended and applied in the non-natural world as well

Eleven-year-old Clay has a name his mother says fits him perfectly. He loves the out-of-doors and prefers activities that keep him close to nature and the land. In school he excels in earth sciences. On weekend camping trips with his scout troop, he can identify almost every plant or animal anyone sees. Each summer, Clay spends a month with his grandparents at the ocean. Here he has amassed a collection of more than five hundred shells. He classifies them in a variety of ways and enjoys making up new categories that are different from the ones he finds in books. Clay has a strong naturalist intelligence.

Characteristics

- involves the ability to recognize flora and fauna
- makes distinctions, comparisons, and contrasts between and among things in the natural world
- oriented toward enjoying outdoor life
- includes the ability to live off the land
- feels comfortable with nature and the natural world
- can create categories and sort and index items accordingly
- organizes in a way that explains and makes things more understandable
- has "street smarts" in an urban environment

Representative Products

- ❑ Science project
- ❑ Chart
- ❑ Experiment
- ❑ Collection of objects
- ❑ Shadow box
- ❑ Terrarium
- ❑ Dissection with notes

Representative Activities

- ❑ Build a school nature trail
- ❑ Conduct experiments and categorize data
- ❑ Create categories to classify information in all subject areas
- ❑ Take a field trip to a nature preserve
- ❑ Use memorization techniques based on putting items in categories
- ❑ Read stories about out-of-door adventures

Representative Careers

- ❑ Zoologist
- ❑ Zookeeper
- ❑ Fisherman
- ❑ Park ranger
- ❑ Wilderness tour guide
- ❑ Forensic scientist
- ❑ Marine biologist
- ❑ Environmental scientist
- ❑ Biological researcher
- ❑ Agricultural experimenter

III. Personal Intelligences

Intrapersonal   **Interpersonal**

Reflects the personal vision each individual has of himself and his relationships with others, and knowledge of cultural norms and social skills in a given society or group

Intrapersonal Intelligence

The ability to have an awareness of, know, and understand one's own hopes, dreams, goals, aspirations, emotions, thoughts, ideas, and convictions. It includes recognition of both strengths and weaknesses and the ability to reflect on one's own life

Trent is quiet and shy, but when he believes in something he will strongly express his feelings. His classmates like Trent because they always know where they stand with him. His best friend describes Trent by saying, "When he says something, you know he's really thought it through." Trent is self confident and likes the quote from Aristotle, 'Know thyself.' He knows both his strengths and weaknesses and works hard to improve in his weak areas. He is a goal setter and when he accomplishes one goal he begins working on another. Trent is well organized and has good time management and study skills. He daydreams quite a bit, thinking of all the possibilities of life. Trent writes down some of his deepest thoughts in a personal poetry journal but doesn't let anyone read it. He would like to be a psychologist when he grows up and has begun to research what types of jobs there might be in that field.

Characteristics

- focuses inward in reflecting upon, analyzing, and understanding one's own feelings and desires
- includes the ability to draw on emotions to direct one's own behavior
- involves the capacity for self-discipline and self-understanding
- uses both strengths and limitations in goal setting, motivation, and planning
- recognizes one's own needs and expectations
- learns from successes and failures
- does not require external approval for actions or convictions
- has strong preferences and is not easily swayed by others
- has good organization, time management, and study skills

Representative Products	Representative Activities	Representative Careers
❑ Autobiography	❑ Independent study	❑ Psychologist
❑ Journal or diary	❑ Journal/poetry writing	❑ Ministry
❑ Reflective poetry	❑ Personal problem solving	❑ Guidance
❑ Interest inventory	❑ Boundary breakers	counselor
❑ Culture poster	❑ Planning long-range projects	❑ Psychiatrist
❑ Assessments of strengths/weaknesses		
❑ Assignment or Agenda notebook		

Interpersonal Intelligence

The ability to sense the moods, feelings, and needs of others, build relationships, display leadership skills, and work collaboratively and effectively as a member of a team

> *Kris and Kim are twins who are in the eighth grade. Everyone likes them, and they seem to have a natural ability to get along with everyone – no matter what their race or ethnic group, and no matter to which clique they belong. The teachers are uniformly positive in their praise of Kris and Kim. They are hard workers in school and do particularly well in group discussions and cooperative learning situations. The girls seem to work better when they can talk about their ideas with others. They are not necessarily the smartest students in the eighth grade, but they are two of the easiest with which to work. The twins are leaders in the Conflict Mediation Team at school and have prevented many fights and interpersonal conflicts throughout the school year.*

Characteristics:

- focuses outward toward others and one's environment

- requires being able to do one's part for the good of the group

- involves the ability to understand and empathize with others

- includes sensitivity to both verbal and nonverbal cues and the ability to respond appropriately to them

- characterized by the ability to perceive the moods, intentions, feelings, and motivations of others

- can persuade others to follow

- asks for, listens to, and considers advice and opinions of others when making a decision

- oriented toward sharing with others

"An intelligence is a biological and psychological potential and is capable of being realized to a greater or lesser extent as a consequence of the experiential, cultural, and motivational factors that affect a person."

Howard Gardner

Representative Products

- ❏ Dialogue
- ❏ Cooperative group project
- ❏ Solutions to problems done in a group
- ❏ Group symbol/logo
- ❏ Persuasive speech
- ❏ Story written by a group
- ❏ Debate
- ❏ Project to help people in the community

Representative Activities

- ❏ Group work
- ❏ Brainstorming
- ❏ E-mailing other people
- ❏ "Talking" on the Internet
- ❏ Pinwheel brainstorming
- ❏ Games for two or more
- ❏ Group problem solving
- ❏ Developing teamwork skills
- ❏ Peer counseling
- ❏ Peer teaching/mentoring
- ❏ Class meeting
- ❏ Class discussion

Representative Careers

- ❏ Salesperson
- ❏ Public relations
- ❏ Politician
- ❏ Teacher
- ❏ Mediator
- ❏ Lawyer

Multiple Intelligences
Student Characteristics

Name at least one of your students with specific strengths in each of the Multiple Intelligences listed below. Include characteristics or behaviors.

Intelligence	Student(s)	Characteristics/Behaviors
Verbal/ Linguistic		
Musical/ Rhythmic		
Logical/ Mathematical		
Visual/ Spatial		
Bodily/ Kinesthetic		
Intrapersonal		
Interpersonal		
Naturalist		

Students' Strengths and Weaknesses in the Multiple Intelligences

It is helpful to be aware of our students' strengths and weaknesses in the Multiple Intelligences. Children usually have strengths in several areas, not just one. Teachers using the Multiple Intelligences can identify strengths and then use these strengths to build up weaker areas.

Sometimes students misbehave because of a weakness in one of the Multiple Intelligences. For example, the student who is always in physical fights with others may have a weakness in Interpersonal intelligence. At the same time, he may be showing his strength in the Bodily/Kinesthetic intelligence, though in a very inappropriate way!

Thomas Armstrong suggests that one good way to identify students' most highly developed intelligences is to observe how they misbehave in class! The child who is always talking when he should not be most likely has highly developed Verbal/Linguistic and Interpersonal intelligences. The child who is always doodling on a piece of paper instead of doing problems in math is probably strong in the Visual/ Spatial intelligence. The student who always seems to have something in his hands to fiddle around with is probably strong in Bodily/Kinesthetic abilities. Although these students are misbehaving in some way, they are all demonstrating their areas of strength.

For too long educators and parents have labeled some children "smart" or "bright" while calling others "dumb" or "stupid" or "slow learners." When adults use these labels, often what may be happening is that the child may be functioning in an intelligence that is unfamiliar or uncomfortable to the teacher or the parent.

Think about typical types of misbehavior in your classroom. Use the **Teacher Reflection Page** on the next page to identify these and the intelligences they may indicate. Sample misbehaviors are listed to help you get started.

"Using Multiple Intelligence theory can greatly affect
students' behaviors in the classroom simply by creating
an environment in which teachers recognize
and attend to individual needs throughout the school day.
Students are less likely to be confused, frustrated or stressed out
in such an environment."

- Thomas Armstrong
"Multiple Intelligences
in the Classroom"

Common Misbehavior in Your Classroom: Which Intelligences Might They Indicate?

Teacher Reflection Page

Type of Misbehavior	Intelligence(s) Indicated	Positive uses of this Intelligence
Always talking	Verbal/Linguistic Interpersonal	Oral report Group discussion
Doodling/drawing	Visual/Spatial	Charts & graphs Posters
Fiddling with objects	Bodily/Kinesthetic	Math manipulatives Constructing a project

Using Multiple Intelligences in Curriculum Planning

The Multiple Intelligence Theory is a good model for designing standards-based curriculum and instruction. Traditionally schools have concentrated heavily on the Verbal/ Linguistic and the Mathematical/Logical intelligences. Because in the 21st century we have a more diverse student population, more diverse needs in the workplace, and more skills necessary for an educated citizenry, we need to use all eight intelligences as tools for curriculum planning as we design learning activities for all students.

Think about which of the Multiple Intelligences you use most often in your teaching and which you try to avoid. Do you use eight different ways of teaching or do you concentrate on just one or two? Do you try to include all eight but just one at a time? Many activities incorporate more than one intelligence. Check yourself with the sample techniques and strategies below. When you plan classroom activities, which of these do you include?

- ❑ Brainstorming (Verbal/Linguistic and Interpersonal)
- ❑ Word games with body movement (Verbal/Linguistic and Bodily/Kinesthetic)
- ❑ Classifying using Venn Diagrams (Logical/Mathematical, Visual/Spatial, and Naturalist)
- ❑ 3 dimensional models/constructions (Visual/Spatial and Bodily/Kinesthetic)
- ❑ Rap and poetry (Verbal/Linguistic, Musical/Rhythmic, and Intrapersonal)
- ❑ Journals (Verbal/Linguistic and Intrapersonal)
- ❑ Cooperative learning (Bodily/Kinesthetic and Interpersonal)
- ❑ Dissecting/taking things apart (Visual/Spatial, Naturalist, and Bodily/Kinesthetic)
- ❑ Graphs and charts (Logical/Mathematical and Visual/Spatial)
- ❑ Hands-on learning (Visual/Spatial and Bodily/Kinesthetic)
- ❑ Creative daydreaming (Visual/Spatial and Intrapersonal)
- ❑ Math concepts set to music (Logical/Mathematical and Musical/Rhythmic)
- ❑ Biology experiments (Naturalist and Bodily/Kinesthetic)

This checklist of sample classroom activities should focus your thinking on how you are using and can use Multiple Intelligences in your classroom. It is essential that teachers consider and include a variety of these Intelligences when planning lessons. Use the **Teacher Reflection** on the next page to list classroom activities you have done, and classify them according to the Multiple Intelligences they address. This will help guide your thinking as you consider how to incorporate Multiple Intelligences Theory into your classroom planning. The **Individualized Lesson Plan™ (ILP)** format works wells with Multiple Intelligences. Offer eight Student Choices, one for each Intelligence. See the sample ILP™ on page 83 and a blank one for you to use to write your own on page 84.

Multiple Intelligences

Teacher Reflection Page

1. List several activities you have done in your class in the past two or three weeks. Indicate the Multiple Intelligence(s) they are most suited for.

Activity:

Multiple Intelligence(s): _____

Activity:

Multiple Intelligence(s): _____

Activity:

Multiple Intelligence(s): _____

Activity:

Multiple Intelligence(s): _____

Activity:

Multiple Intelligence(s): _____

2. Which of the intelligences do most of your classroom activities focus on?

3. Which intelligences are most difficult for you to work with?

4. Use the Individual Lesson Plan (ILP)™ form on page 84 to plan a Student Choice activity for each of the multiple intelligences that you could use in a unit of study.

INDIVIDUAL LESSON PLAN - MULTIPLE INTELLIGENCES

ACTIVITIES - STUDENT CHOICES

Verbal/Linguistic
1. Write a short story showing how inventions have helped us send messages from person to person. Include telegraph, telephone, e-mail and fax.

Musical/Rhythmic
5. Find a song that relates to an invention. Listen to it and list what you can learn about the invention from the song.

Logical/Mathematical
2. Make a list of various inventions that measure things. What does each measure and what types of measurements are used? Show your answers on a chart or an outline.

Visual/Spatial
6. Draw a comic strip illustrating the development of the camera from the first cameras in the 1800s to the digital cameras of today.

Bodily/Kinesthetic
3. Demonstrate how the following inventions work: chiming clock, alarm clock, cuckoo clock, pendulum clock, and digitized clock or watch.

Naturalist
7. Research ways inventions have harmed the natural environment. Make an album or scrapbook of 'before and after' pictures to show the harm that has been done.

Intrapersonal
4. Thomas Edison once said, "Genius is 1% inspiration and 99% perspiration." Write a reflection paper explaining what this quote means to you.

Interpersonal
8. With a group of classmates, think of an everyday problem that might be solved through a new invention. Brainstorm possibilities and make a diagram or drawing of your new invention.

Required Activities — Teacher's Choice
1. Read background information on a variety of types of inventions from textbook. List each with important facts.
2. Choose one category of invention and trace its development from the time of its beginning until the present. Use a time line or diagram with written details.
3. Write a short story about life without an invention of your choice.

Product/Performance — Required
1. List facts

2. Time line or diagram

3. Short story

Assessment — Required Activities
1. Accuracy
   At least 2 facts for each

2. Correct sequence
   Visual is clear

3. Structure and mechanics
   Organization
   Creativity

Optional Student-Parent Cooperative Activity

Student Choices in Ways to Learn
Verbal/Linguistic

Musical/Rhythmic

Logical/Mathematical

Visual/Spatial

Bodily/Kinesthetic

Naturalist

Intrapersonal

Interpersonal

Product/Performance — Student Choice

Standards

Due Date — Student Choice

INDIVIDUAL LESSON PLAN - MULTIPLE INTELLIGENCES

Assessment Required Activities	Product/Performance Required	Required Activities Teacher's Choice

Standards		

Due Date Student Choice	Product/Performance Student Choice	Optional Student-Parent Cooperative Activity

Student Choices in Ways to Learn

Verbal/Linguistic _____

Musical/Rhythmic _____

Logical/Mathematical _____

Visual/Spatial _____

Bodily/Kinesthetic _____

Naturalist _____

Intrapersonal _____

Interpersonal _____

ACTIVITIES - STUDENT CHOICES

Musical/Rhythmic	Verbal/Linguistic

Visual/Spatial	Logical/Mathematical

Naturalist	Bodily/Kinesthetic

Interpersonal	Intrapersonal

Compare and Contrast

Teacher Reflection Page

Learning Modalities and Multiple Intelligences have some similarities yet are different in many ways. Use this Venn diagram to record your ideas as you contrast the two.

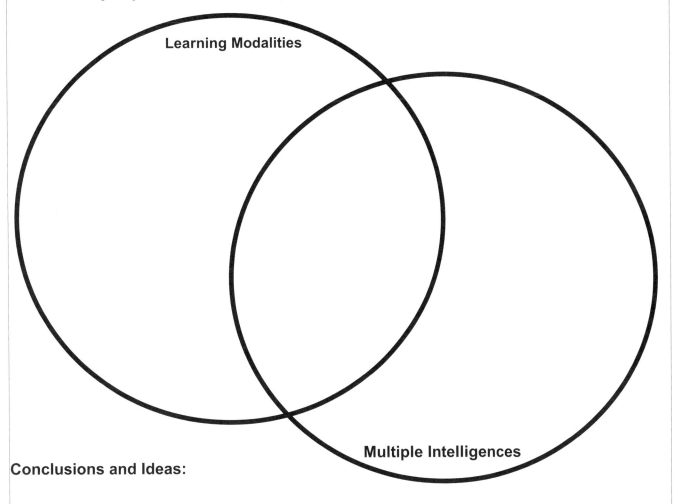

Conclusions and Ideas:

Reflections

* Intelligence can be defined in many different ways.

* Howard Gardner's Theory of Multiple Intelligence states there are at least eight types of Intelligence:

- Verbal/Linguistic

- Musical/Rhythmic

- Logical/Mathematical

- Visual/Spatial

- Bodily/Kinesthetic

- Interpersonal

- Naturalist

* Intelligence can be developed and taught. It is not one fixed number assigned in early childhood and kept for life.

* All students have strengths and weaknesses in the Multiple Intelligence.

* Multiple Intelligence can be used in curriculum planning in several different ways.

Notes _____

Chapter 6

Assessment

Questions to Consider

1. Why are standardized tests considered so important in most school districts?

2. What data do standardized tests provide?

3. What is meant by assessment?

4. What are some alternative ways to assess students?

5. How is alternative assessment linked with instruction?

The Impact of No Child Left Behind (NCLB) on Assessment

The *No Child Left Behind Act (NCLB)* went into effect in 2002. Because this law requires yearly testing of all students in most grade levels, it has created enormous pressure to raise test scores. One goal of the law is to close the achievement gap among students, including rich and poor, white and minority, regular education and special education, native English speaking and English language learners.

As of this writing, the law stipulates that test score data be broken out, or disaggregated, by student subgroups according to race, ethnicity, gender, English language proficiency, disabilities, and income level. Schools are required to test at least 95% of students in each subgroup and to show adequate yearly progress (AYP) in every subgroup. There are severe consequences for schools not making AYP with all of their students. Thus, testing and test preparation have become a major emphasis in nearly every American school.

I have worked with teachers and students in many school districts on test-taking skills. Without exception, I have found dedicated, worried teachers and administrators who are concerned that their students won't do well (or haven't done well in the past) on the high-stakes required standardized tests. These educators want to do everything possible to prepare their students in test-taking skills and ensure that their students will be successful.

While there are several strategies we can use to develop test-taking skills, I wonder about this large national frenzy regarding standardized test scores. There are some basic questions we need to ask ourselves about testing, assessment, and evaluation. What is the real purpose of assessment? What sorts of evaluative information do we need about each student? How often should we assess students and report on their progress?

Standardized Tests: Importance and Pitfalls

NCLB has made standardized testing an important and widely recognized instrument for measuring student learning across the United States. It is seen as a means of addressing accountability and determining educational progress, and is considered so important because it has the power to change children's lives. As a society, we constantly compare children to one another via their test scores.

Tests can determine which classes students will take, which schools they will attend, and their academic potential. They have a powerful influence on what goes on in the classroom. In many school districts, passing the standardized test is the ticket to promotion to the next grade level or to graduation itself.

Tests influence school goals, dominate instruction, and reflect teacher performance. In some programs, they are the deciding factor in establishing levels of program funding. Newspapers print test scores on the front page, comparing one school or school district with another. Realtors use them to recommend the best school or school district in which to live. And they are one means through which university researchers identify effective schools and with which high school students gain admittance to higher education.

When so much time is spent on testing, the opportunities for student learning in other areas sometimes become more limited. In many schools, students have less time to develop strengths and interest areas because they are spending more and more time in drill and practice sessions for multiple-choice exams. As a result, getting the right answer has become the goal and convergent thinking the norm. Divergent thinking and creativity have been de-emphasized. Many tests minimize the ambiguity of tasks and answers; thus, test items tend to be deliberately simplified. Unfortunately, students' abilities to use knowledge critically or creatively are not assessed well in this process. In fact, "thinking" test takers often defeat themselves by looking too far below the surface of the questions, and end up scoring lower than they should.

Testing is the mode of assessment that is weakest in showing students' true strengths and creative capacities. Yet, standardized tests can provide us with some information about student learning. They do provide standardized data that educators can use to assess student progress from one year to the next. They also provide a means of national, state, and school-wide comparisons in a country where education is so fragmented and localized. Additionally, they sample content effectively and can be scored quickly.

Because these tests have taken on such importance, teaching to the test has become more and more common. The result has been rising test scores without comparable demonstrations that the students are really learning significantly.

Nevertheless, it appears that the importance of standardized testing will probably not diminish any time soon. For the foreseeable future, it will be with us in one form or another. Skills in studying for and taking tests are essential for success in today's schools. Therefore, you must include these skills in the repertoire of skills you teach your students. Here are some suggestions:

- **Share every test-taking tip you know.**

- **Demystify tests for your students. Many students think test items come out of thin air. Show them how tests are constructed.**

- **Encourage your students to study for tests together or to study with their parents.**

- **Find out ways to lessen test anxiety for your students.**

- **Share your own strategies and "tricks of the trade" for test taking and test making.**

- **Have your students write their own tests and quizzes for classroom tests.**

For more information on Test Taking Skills, including *Dealing with Test Anxiety, Memorization Techniques, Time Management, Making Correct Choices on Multiple Choice Tests,* and *Taking Essay Exams,* see **Motivating Underachievers** and **Becoming an Achiever** by Carolyn Coil, Pieces of Learning.

Performance Assessment vs Assessment through Testing

Two philosophies of student assessment seem to coexist in American education at the present time. Many educators advocate assessing student performance in context through various means of authentic or performance assessment, a process where students show what they know through products, performances, or portfolios of their work. Many other stakeholders in the educational system feel that the best way to see what students have learned is to use large-scale generic tests. This kind of testing assumes that knowledge can be decomposed into small elements and that it can be known out of context. The tension between these two beliefs about assessment and education can be felt in almost every school district in our country.

Many tests given to students provide a means for us to judge content knowledge and skills, but they tend to bear little relationship to the real practice of the subject. Right and wrong multiple choice tests are not very much like real life. They are inherently restricted to unambiguous items, whereas real life is filled with ambiguity. In real life we use our intellect, knowledge, and skills in a given situation to solve a certain problem. There is a difference between taking a test where there is one right answer and completing a product or performance where a variety of knowledge and skills are used to respond to the particular task at hand. A product or performance is done in context and involves constant judgment in adapting knowledge.

In a testing situation, students are handicapped in their access to factual knowledge or sources of information as compared to real life. When students take a test, they generally are not allowed access to their notes, reference materials, or human resources. All they can use are the facts they have managed to memorize. A standardized test therefore cannot show how students sift through all the facts, synthesize information, or use knowledge to good effect. Certainly in real life this is never the case. I would hate to be writing this book, for instance, without access to notes, reference materials, and a host of human resources! Why not allow students to bring their notes to a test if our aim is to see what they understand, not just what they have managed to memorize for the short term?

Assessment is the **process of collecting and organizing information or data so that it can be judged or evaluated.** It should include all the processes we use for gathering information about student learning to meet a variety of evaluation needs. Assessment data becomes an indicator of what and how students are learning. It should include a variety of strategies and procedures. We assess students through tests, but they are only one part of the assessment process. In the next portion of this chapter, we will look more closely at alternative assessment methods.

Keep in mind — Student assessment is much more than test taking!

Assessment

Teacher Reflection Page

Think about some of the issues regarding assessment which are paramount in your own school and school district. Reflect on the questions below with at least one of your colleagues.

1. How much time do you spend in preparing your students for standardized tests?

2. What connections do you see between the content covered on the tests and the curriculum you are teaching?

3. How can you help demystify the testing process for your students?

4. In which test taking skills are your students strong? What are their weaknesses? How can you help them work on these?

5. How open are you to using various alternative methods of assessment? Does the school administration support alternative assessment? Do the parents understand it?

6. What problems do you see in using alternative assessment? What advantages do you feel alternative assessment has over traditional methods of assessing students?

Three Important Types of Assessments

There are three major types of assessments that are useful in the classroom. All three should be aligned with curricular and instructional objectives and with state standards. They are:

- Pre-assessments

- Formative assessments

- Summative assessments

Most rubrics and checklists can be used as formative assessments, summative assessments, or both. Pre-assessment is usually done via a pretest, student observation, a checklist, or some other evidence of past work and knowledge. Summative assessments can be performance assessments, tests, or both.

Pre-assessment is . . .

Any method, strategy, or process used to determine a student's current level of readiness or interest in order to plan for appropriate instruction.

- Provides data and information that can determine learning options or levels for students in a differentiated classroom

- Helps teachers understand the nature of learning differences in his/her students before planning instruction

- Allows students to demonstrate mastery or to show where remediation might be needed before instruction begins

Formative Assessment is . . .

The process of accumulating information about a student's progress while he or she is working on a learning task. This helps in making ongoing instructional decisions during a unit of work.

It gives teachers information about what their students are doing so that they can change, modify, or extend the instructional activities. Teachers can use this information to make adjustments to their instruction as they teach, and students can self-assess and improve as they learn. It is assessment **for** learning rather than assessment **of** learning.

- Alerts the teacher early on about student misconceptions or lack of understanding about what is being studied

- Allows students to change and improve their work before turning it in for the final grade

- Provides regular feedback to student

- Provides evidence of progress in learning and points to the next steps in the learning process

Summative Assessment is . . .

A means to determine a student's mastery of information, knowledge, skills, concepts, etc. after the unit or learning activity has been completed.

- Should parallel the formative assessments that were used during the learning process

- May determine an exit grade or score and can be tied to a final decision about a student

- Should align with instructional/curricular objectives, standards, and benchmarks

- May be a form of alternative assessment; doesn't always have to be a test

Types of Assessment

Teacher Reflection Questions

1. Which of these three types of assessment do you use the most? Why?

2. Give examples of ways pre-assessments can be helpful and useful in the classroom.

3. How and why do formative assessments help in raising student achievement? What has been your experience in using them?

4. Do you think summative assessments are overly emphasized in schools? Why or why not?

Authentic Assessment Methods: Alternatives to Tests

Some terms you may hear when assessment is discussed include "authentic," "alternative," and "performance" assessments. These terms are used more or less interchangeably to indicate types of assessment strategies that go beyond paper-and-pencil testing and are linked more directly to the purposes and meaning of what is taught rather than on testing specific skills and knowledge. They usually get closer to assessing what students are actually learning because they are rooted in student performance on various learning tasks.

Performance assessment includes projects, products, or performances that are used to exhibit those things students have learned. Performance assessments should be linked to learning the standards and demonstrate that learning in a concrete way. Some indicators are the following:

- Students know they have learned something when they can explain their work and ideas to others or when they can successfully teach others difficult concepts or content.

- Students know they have learned something when they are able to apply the knowledge to new problems or situations.

- Students know they have learned something when they create projects that actually work.

Alternative assessment methods go hand-in-hand with standards-based curriculum and educational reforms in schools. There is a close connection between alternative assessments and classroom instruction. 75% of students who are involved in performance assessment tasks say they prefer them over more traditional forms of assessment such as tests and written reports. They feel performance assessments allow people to see what they are really capable of doing and help them think for themselves. They also state that such assessments require more maturity, ownership, and self motivation on the part of the student and a great deal more work.

Alternative assessment includes products and/or performances along with at least one of the following:

- Portfolios of student work

- Student logs recording steps in the completion of a task

- Classroom discussions for sharing student work, examining strategies for improving it, and evaluating it in terms of what they like and dislike

- Peer response sessions and interviews in which students make thoughtful responses about their work

- Formal reflections where students review their past work and reflect on their growth and learning over time. These serve as evidence of evolving strengths and weaknesses

- Checklists and rating scales

- Rubrics and Criteria Cards

Linking Assessment with Instruction

Alternative forms of assessment differ quite dramatically from paper-pencil tests. One of the goals of assessment is to enhance the teaching and learning process. This means assessment and evaluation should be contextualized; that is, rooted in instructional programs, not apart from them. When assessment measures are specific and relate directly to school and classroom-based instruction, students tend to be more successful and assessment outcomes tend to be higher.

Performance or authentic assessments serve as a connection between instruction and assessment. They provide a means through which instruction and assessment can be woven together. Projects and performances link easily with instruction. They usually have a meaningful context in which knowledge is used in a setting important to the student. In this way, such assessment tasks encourage higher-level thinking processes where knowledge and skills are applied in a new situation.

Many of the products and performances used in the **Individual Lesson Plan**™ **(ILP)** format in this book are good examples of authentic assessment tasks. They are tied directly to classroom instruction yet can also be used for assessment. Designing performance assessment tasks such as these will help you to focus on what you expect students to know and what outcomes and competencies you are teaching toward. Authentic assessments highlight student work and should promote high-quality performance. This approach usually aligns assessment and instruction because there is an effort to match assessment to student work.

Designing Performance Assessment Tasks

Picture a group of students in front of a panel of teachers, parents, and experts presenting and discussing their portfolios and demonstrating their projects that show they have met the school's standards and learning outcomes in a particular area. The criteria for assessing and evaluating their work has been established and is understood by all involved. Each student's work will be self-assessed as well as involved in peer assessment, teacher assessment, and feedback from an outside expert. Such students are engaged in the final activity of an authentic performance assessment task.

In order to design performance assessment tasks, teachers must first look at their standards to see what their students should be able to know and do. Then they need to decide what learning activities students must experience in order for them to demonstrate this knowledge in some way. To accomplish this, teachers must think through the curriculum content to establish learning outcomes or objectives, design performance activities that will allow students to demonstrate their achievement of these outcomes, and specify criteria by which they will be evaluated.

Some examples of performance samples used for assessment include writing, drawing, computations, constructions, and projects. Designing performance assessment tasks helps teachers to focus on what they are expecting students to know and what standards they are teaching. Performance assessments highlight student work and should promote high-quality performance. This approach usually aligns assessment and instruction because there is an effort to match assessment to student work.

Alternative assessment is much more time consuming than traditional assessment! However, the results can show us much more about student learning than more traditional assessments do. Following is a more detailed examination of some of the more common types of alternative assessment.

Performance Assessment Tools

Four elements of an effective performance assessment task include:

- A meaningful context in which knowledge is used in a setting important to the student
- Higher-level thinking processes where knowledge and skills are applied in a new situation
- An appropriate product or performance that demonstrates understanding of the standards
- A well-constructed rubric or checklist that serves as a guide in doing the task and in evaluating student work

Performance assessment tasks can be assessed and evaluated using a variety of assessment tools. These include

Video Assessment Records	**Portfolios**	**Checklists**	**Rubrics**
Criteria Cards	**Observations**	**Rating Scales**	**Mini-Rubrics**

Video Assessment Records Performance assessments need to include ways for students to reflect about their learning. One way to do this is to make a video of student performances and presentations for study and evaluation. This allows students to see things they were not aware of during the performance. During group work, videos can also show collaboration (or lack thereof) between various students, including who dominates the group and who does not speak up. A video of a performance assessment can be used as a reflective tool. With video records of various performance assessments, students can develop new insights about their work. They can also examine how their knowledge and skills have grown during the school year.

Portfolios are **a representative collection of students' work which has been done over a period of time.** They are a means of documenting student learning and showing persons outside of the classroom what has been accomplished in school. Portfolios provide a way to show individual student growth and achievement by exhibiting a range of work.

Portfolios offer the opportunity to observe students in a broader context than traditional assessment can. In addition to assessing products and performances, portfolios can also assess process skills. For example, depending upon what is chosen for the portfolio, it can show the amount of risk-taking that was done by the student in choosing a product or activity. The student who always chooses the easiest or least challenging project may need to reflect on how to be more of a risk taker. Portfolios can also show leadership characteristics, how well a student works with others, and time management and organizational skills. Criteria reflecting growth in these skills can be part of a student log, checklist, or portfolio assessment form.

Portfolios have been called the "intersection of instruction and assessment" because they provide a means through which instruction and assessment can be woven together. Portfolios require students to collect and reflect upon examples of their own work and make choices about which is representative of their knowledge and learning. In this way, they encourage students to become participants in their own assessment. Think through your own use of portfolios by considering the questions on the next page.

Things to Consider When Using Portfolios

Teacher Reflection Page

Before using portfolios with your students, it is best to discuss these issues and concerns with them:

What will it look like?

How will it be structured?

What should go in it?

What will best show progress toward learning goals?

Will it show only the best work (showcase portfolio) or will it show work which documents improvement?

How and when will work samples be selected for the portfolio?

What standards will be demonstrated in the portfolio?

How much will the portfolio be counted in the final assessment, grade, or evaluation of the work done in the class?

How will evaluation criteria reflect standards of excellence, effort, and growth?

What type of assessment instrument will be used to assess items in the portfolio?

How will the work in the portfolio be shared with parents? With other adults in the community? With other students?

Observations, Checklists, and Rating Scales

Observations, checklists, and rating scales are often built upon the formal and informal assessment practices teachers already use. Teachers who work with students on a daily basis intuitively know their students, can understand their questions, and can address their growth as learners. These assessment measures provide a way to document student growth and record information that teachers note about a child informally on a regular basis.

Observational records come in various shapes, types, and sizes. Some examples are rating forms, narrative descriptions, checklists, logs, and anecdotes. They help students and teachers recognize strengths and weaknesses and point the way to develop strategies for improvement. Formal observations help teachers find out if a child has learned certain things and often show other aspects of student growth teacher may otherwise have missed. They also may include notes on interests, behavior, thinking, social skills, study skills, and relationships.

Informal folders and inventories such as checklists provide necessary documentation and give teachers a way to keep records about students' work. They facilitate a way to keep track of student activities and what each student has been involved in. Some sample reproducible checklists used to identify students' affective and academic strengths and weaknesses can be found on the next four pages. Two are appropriate for K-3 students and two for grades 4 and above.

Use these and also design your own checklists to help you keep accurate records of skills, content knowledge, or affective areas.

Academic Characteristics of Students
Who Are Becoming Achievers

1. Rate your strengths and weaknesses in these areas.
2. Check **S** for each of your strengths.
3. Then count the number of **S's**.
4. Check **W** for weaknesses, but do not check more **W's** than **S's**.
5. You may leave some items blank!

<u>S</u>	<u>W</u>	
_____	_____	I love reading.
_____	_____	I do well in at least one part of schoolwork.
_____	_____	I can do math well.
_____	_____	I always have my school supplies.
_____	_____	I come to school on time.
_____	_____	I listen to the teacher.
_____	_____	I ask my teacher for help.
_____	_____	School is important to me.
_____	_____	I like art and music.
_____	_____	I like to work with my hands.
_____	_____	I learn new things every day.

Personal Characteristics of Students
Who Are Becoming Achievers

1. Rate your strengths and weaknesses in these areas.
2. Check **S** for each of your strengths.
3. Then count the number of **S's**.
4. Check **W** for weaknesses, but do not check more **W's** than **S's**.
5. You may leave some items blank!

S   **W**

_____ _____   I like myself.

_____ _____   I say, "I can do it!" even when it's hard.

_____ _____   I like school.

_____ _____   I love my teacher.

_____ _____   I have friends who like school.

_____ _____   I follow the rules.

_____ _____   I think I learn a lot in school.

_____ _____   I ask for help when I need it.

_____ _____   I share with others.

_____ _____   I treat other people kindly.

_____ _____   I have a special interest area.

Academic Characteristics of Students Who Are Becoming Achievers

Rate your strengths and weaknesses in these areas. Check S for each of your strengths. Then count the number of S's. Check W for weaknesses, but do not check more W's than S's. You may leave some items blank.

S   W

____   ____ I feel that at least one subject/topic/class in school is interesting and worthwhile.

____   ____ I have good organizational and time management skills.

____   ____ I am able to comprehend reading assignments in the subjects I take.

____   ____ I find it easy to memorize unfamiliar information.

____   ____ I like to have high quality in my schoolwork.

____   ____ I keep working and don't give up on subjects that don't come easily.

____   ____ I pay attention and am able to concentrate on assignments.

____   ____ I come to school on time and have good attendance.

____   ____ I am willing to get help on subjects or assignments I don't understand.

____   ____ I work to improve when my grades or test scores are low.

____   ____ I set short and long-term goals for myself.

____   ____ In some subjects, I want to do more than just "get by."

____   ____ I am a creative person.

____   ____ I know that doing well in school will help me in the future.

*From **Becoming An Achiever** by Carolyn Coil. Pieces of Learning, Marion IL*

Personal Characteristics of Students Who Are Becoming Achievers

Rate your strengths and weaknesses in these areas. Check S for each of your strengths. Then count the number of S's. Check W for weaknesses, but do not check more W's than S's. You may leave some items blank!

S   W

____ ____ I have confidence in myself.

____ ____ I let my teachers know when I am having a problem and work with them in problem solving.

____ ____ I am a risk taker.

____ ____ I am willing to work to make changes in myself.

____ ____ I listen to those in authority over me.

____ ____ I take responsibility for my problems and do not put all of the blame on others.

____ ____ I work well in a group which is working on a constructive project.

____ ____ I have a close friend or friends who share similar positive interests.

____ ____ I am flexible and can see more than one possible solution when solving a problem.

____ ____ I have an area of special interest.

____ ____ I practice self-discipline and self-control.

____ ____ I use my influence over others in a positive way.

____ ____ I have a positive attitude toward school.

____ ____ I know when I have contributed to a behavior problem or conflict.

____ ____ My friends are achievers and have positive attitudes about school.

____ ____ I try to have appropriate behavior.

*From **Becoming An Achiever** by Carolyn Coil. Pieces of Learning, Marion IL*

Using Rubrics and Developing Assessment Criteria

Rubrics

A rubric is a set of scoring guidelines for assessing student work. A typical rubric:

- Contains a scale of different possible points or levels to be assigned for varying degrees of mastery

- States the different traits or criteria to be examined in the product or performance

- Provides pointers for assessing each of the traits and finding the right place on the scoring scale to which a particular student's work corresponds

Rubrics are especially beneficial because nearly all student projects, products, and performances can be assessed in a multitude of ways. It is up to the teacher to determine the significant learning outcomes for each type of student work. This provides a focus and direction for the student, and it also gives the teacher a concrete way to decide on the criteria that will best assess what each student does.

One of the most difficult tasks for teachers who use alternative assessment methods is developing assessment criteria. It is difficult partly because it seems to be quite subjective. There can be a lot of conscious or unconscious bias in this type of assessment, thus we must make sure that the criteria is fair. Rubrics help us to clearly define assessment criteria.

When working on different performance assessment tasks, students should know exactly what the criteria is and teachers ought to be teaching directly to the criteria if the outcomes of the task are worthwhile. Assessment criteria for performance assessments should never be a mystery to the students. No student should ever have to muse: *"I wonder how the teacher is going to grade this project?"* Instead, students should be able to tell anyone who asks exactly what the assessment criteria is. In fact, in this situation, teaching toward the assessment becomes a goal.

Developing assessment criteria is complicated. Assessing complex tasks requires complex assessment criteria, with each part of the task having its own set of criteria. Assessment criteria must be specific and detailed, carefully defined, clear, and easily communicated. One way to start is to look at generic lists of criteria for various tasks, performances, or products and then adapt them to meet the specific needs of your content and your students.

When developing a rubric, think carefully about the standards you are hoping your students will master. Then brainstorm all possible criteria you might want to consider in assessing the stated learning outcomes. If you have an exceptionally long list, it may be necessary to pare down your list or to combine two or more of your criteria into one item.

Sometimes you will have criteria that are consistent no matter what the topic or assignment. These generally will be generic **processes** you often want students to focus on or **products/performances** your students may do several different times or for different teachers.

Processes could include writing conventions such as grammar, spelling, punctuation, or sentence structure, or a skill like proofreading, research skills, or organizational skills. It might even be expected classroom behaviors such as turning in work on time or group work expectations. The list of generic products and performances could be unending. Look in the back of this book for a sampling.

In any of these cases, you can develop **Product** or **Process Criteria Cards** to use over and over again as you write rubrics or give students assessment criteria in other ways. These cards have short, easily understood lists of criteria (generally 3-5) that students can use each time they use the same process or complete the same product. If all teachers at a given grade level or within a certain department agree to use the same Criteria Cards, students would benefit greatly from the consistency.

For example, if the teacher wants students to write a short paper and complete a diagram of a one-celled animal, she could use a Proofreading Criteria Card (Process) and a Diagram Criteria Card (Product) as part of criteria for this activity. If students had a copy of the Criteria Cards, she would indicate 'Follow Proofreading Criteria Card' and 'Follow Diagram Criteria Card' as two items in the assessment criteria.

Proofreading	**Diagram**
1. First draft is read carefully	1. Object or process is drawn accurately
2. Mistakes in spelling, punctuation and grammar are noted	2. Parts are labeled correctly
3. Mistakes are corrected on final copy	3. Clear and neat
	4. Shows relationships between parts or ideas

There are no rules about how many criteria you need to have or how many levels need to be indicated in a rubric. In general, four or five levels is maximum. The same is true for the number of criteria listed. The more levels and the more criteria, the more cumbersome the rubric becomes. From a practical standpoint, most students stop reading rubrics or directions when they are too complex or too wordy.

In addition, extremely long rubrics are difficult for teachers to use. If the purpose of a rubric is to give feedback to the student, facilitate self-assessment, and/or to help the teacher accurately and fairly score a piece of student work, the rubric should be as simple and understandable as possible.

In a rubric with five levels, the levels might indicate the following:

1 = The task was attempted but falls far short of quality work.

2 = Important purposes were not achieved. The product or performance needs more work, redirection or additional strategies.

3 = For the most part, the task was accomplished. Needs minor corrections, additions or changes.

4 = The task was fully accomplished and done well.

5 = This work is above and beyond requirements and far exceeds expectations. It shows creative and unique thinking, the ability to problem solve and/or unusual skill in any of the multiple intelligences.

The top level in any rubric should be the extension column. That is, it should provide a way to show that a student has extended his/her learning above and beyond the assigned task or expectations. This is particularly important for gifted and talented and other high ability students. We do not want them to stop learning once they have reached the minimum expectation for a project or performance! A better idea is to continue to challenge them and to indicate this within the rubric itself.

A good rubric helps teachers grade all types of products and performances more fairly since rubrics require teachers to be much more precise about what their expectations are. Rubrics give students an understanding of the meaning behind the grade. Rubrics can be developed by the teacher or by the students. Developing the rubric is a great way to show students what makes an excellent project or performance.

Most schools, school districts, and state departments of education have rubrics for various alternative assessment tasks. Web sites that allow you to construct rubrics such as

www.4teachers.org/techalong (RubiStar)

are also good sources of information about rubrics. Become familiar with these, and then adapt them to best meet your needs.

Guidelines for a Good Rubric

- Is understandable to the student

- Can be used by the student as a guide for doing quality work

- Challenges students to go beyond expectations

- Can be used by the teacher to grade or assess coherently and fairly

- Can be used to defend the grade if questioned by a student or a parent

Complex Rubrics and Mini-Rubrics

Two useful types of rubrics are **Complex Rubrics** and **Mini-Rubrics**. Complex rubrics have criteria, columns to indicate various levels, and descriptors of each level in small boxes within the rubric. These are essential to use in assessing an important piece of student work, especially when it is a Teacher Required activity and all students are doing the same task.

However, when you give students a number of choices of activities, it is usually not practical or feasible to write a complex rubric for each student choice. When using the **Individual Lesson Plan**™ **(ILP)**, students could have 8-12 different choices. For these, I recommend using mini-rubrics. These are short lists of assessment criteria that can be written on the back of the **ILP**™ form. Students can read the criteria before making a choice of activities to work on and these same criteria can help guide their work. They also provide a quick way for teachers to grade the student choice activities. Extensions can be included in mini-rubrics and serve the same function in challenging high ability students as the extension column does in a complex rubric.

On the next four pages, you will find assessments to use with the **ILP**™ on page 65:

- A sample complex rubric for a Time Line of Inventions

- A blank rubric form for your use

- Mini-rubrics for assessing the 8 Student Choice activities

- A blank mini-rubric form for your use

You will see that a **Time Line Criteria Card** is embedded into the complex rubric:

Time Line Criteria Card

1. **Title/events spelled correctly**

2. **Chronological order**

3. **Well-plotted time spans**

4. **Neat and legible**

RUBRIC FOR Time Line of Ten Most Important Inventions

NAME: DATE:

CRITERIA	1	2	3	4	5 Extension
Inventions are listed on Time Line	5 or less inventions are listed	6-7 inventions are listed	8-9 inventions are listed	10 inventions are listed	Has more than 10; includes unique ideas or inventions
Accurate date and name of inventor indicated for each invention	Has 5 or less dates and inventors OR 6-9 but 5+ are inaccurate	Has 6-9 dates and inventors and at least 6 are accurate	Has all 10 dates and inventors but 1-3 are inaccurate	All 10 dates and inventors are accurate	Has more than 10; includes extra information about inventor
Includes other important facts	Has one fact each for 5 different inventions	Has one fact each for 6-9 inventions	Has one fact each for all 10 inventions	Has facts for all 10 inventions and more than one for some	Has facts for 10 or more and indicates importance of each invention for student
Follows Time Line criteria card	Has one item on the criteria card	Has 2 items on the criteria card	Has 3 items on the criteria card	Has all 4 items on the criteria card	Wow! Has all 4 items plus a beautifully illustrated time line that could go in a book!
Points					
Total points					Grade

DATE:

RUBRIC FOR
NAME:

CRITERIA	1	2	3	4	5

CLC0378 Pieces of Learning

Assessment of Student Choices – Individual Lesson Plan on page 65

1. Model of Invention (Application)
- Sturdy and durable model
- Clearly shows how homework is done
- Creativity
- Oral or written explanation telling how it works

Possible points = _____

2. List with Functions (Application)
- Lists 20 household inventions
- Indicates functions of each invention
- Explains how function would be done without the invention

Suggested extension: Combine two of the inventions on your list that then could perform a new function.

Possible points = _____

3. Diagram and Explanation (Analysis)
- Follows Diagram criteria card
- Diagram clearly shows interactions between parts
- Clear written explanation
- Correct spelling and punctuation

Possible points = _____

4. List with Suggestions (Analysis)
- Lists 5 or more inventions
- Indicates harm to environment done by each
- Has suggestions for improvement for each

Suggested extension: Create a new invention that helps the environment.

Possible points = _____

5. Design of House (Synthesis)
- Design shows flow of heat and cold in house
- Alternate energy source identified and explained
- How alternate energy source works is clear
- Drawing is clear, neat, and has appropriate labels

Possible points = _____

6. Short Story (Synthesis)
- Story has a beginning, middle, and end
- Changes in life are part of the story itself
- Characters experience changes
- At least five changes are included

Possible points = _____

7. Position Paper (Evaluation)
- Position paper clearly identifies invention
- Five logical reasons are given
- Explains what life would be like without the invention

Suggested extension: Do a skit or role play showing life without this invention.

Possible points = _____

8. List with Reasons (Evaluation)
- Inventor and three events are clearly identified
- Reasons these three events are significant are given
- Includes a list of three or more sources of information

Suggested extension: Compare and contrast events in this inventor's life with events in your own life. Explain why events in your own life may be significant in the future.

Possible points = _____

Assessment of Student Choices – Individual Lesson Plan –

1. • • • •
_____
Possible points = _____

2. • • • •
_____
Possible points = _____

3. • • • •
_____
Possible points = _____

4. • • • •
_____
Possible points = _____

5. • • • •
_____
Possible points = _____

6. • • • •
_____
Possible points = _____

7. • • • •
_____
Possible points = _____

8. • • • •
_____
Possible points = _____

Assessing Creativity

Many teachers have difficulty in assessing products or performances where creativity is the major outcome or learning goal. Below are some guidelines you may wish to use in assessing elements of the creative process.

Guidelines for Assessing Elements of the Creative Process

When assessing creativity or elements of the creative process, incorporate the guidelines below.

→ **Fluency**

- The number of ideas generated

- The number of ideas generated within a certain time

- The increase in the number of ideas generated within a certain time

→ **Flexibility**

- The number of different categories of ideas generated

- The number of times the categories change

→ **Originality**

- The uniqueness of the idea, performance,or product as compared to others in the class or group

- The uniqueness of the idea, performance, or product as compared to what this student has done in the past

→ **Elaboration**

- The number of details provided in one response

- The complexity of a product or performance

- The number of sources and ideas used and synthesized into the final product or performance

→ **Divergent Thinking**

- The number of plausible answers to the same question

- The number of alternative solutions to a given problem

Reporting Student Progress

> *"How many points will I get for doing this activity? I have to make sure I get enough to bring my report card grade up to a B."*
>
> *"Does this count? If it doesn't, why do I have to do it?"*
>
> *"Is this assignment going to be graded? How much will it count toward our final grade in this class?"*

Many of the questions students and their parents ask center around points and grades with little focus on the learning itself. When we only report numbers, letters, or test scores, students and parents come to believe these are the only things that are important.

This viewpoint is affirmed by the reaction of our culture. Children are asked about their report card grades and often are paid for the As they receive. College scholarships are frequently awarded based on test scores and grade point averages.

NCLB requires schools be labeled as 'Needs Improvement,' 'Corrective Action,' or 'Restructuring' based on test scores received by students in the school. It is little wonder that most parents, students, and teachers are focused on points and scores!

Consider another approach in the quotes below.

> *"When I bring my report card home, my mom sees what I liked in school and what I did well in. It helps me tell her more about school."*
>
> *"Goal setting on my report card is really good. It focuses me on what I want to do next."*
>
> *"I can't wait to get my report card! I get to write about three of my strengths and the special project I am going to work on during my next independent study."*
>
> *"Look at all the standards I've mastered!"*

The above quotes come from actual students who receive standards-based, anecdotal report cards in addition to letter grades. Report cards, newsletters, and conferences can be used along with various forms of authentic assessments to convey student progress to parents. Reporting to parents should include not only number or letter grades but also references to the standards, extensive teacher comments, student self-assessments, year long goals for achievement, action plans for future learning, and evaluations of each student's strengths and weaknesses.

Alternative assessment methods lead to exciting new ways of communicating with parents and including them in the educational process. Anecdotal report cards with teacher-developed comments can clearly and consistently describe each student's progress in relation to the curriculum. Student-created report cards encourage students to self assess their performance and set new goals for learning. Standards-based report cards show students and parents exactly which standards they have mastered and which they still need to work on.

Student-led conferences in which students review their work for their parents and teacher gives them an opportunity to demonstrate their knowledge. This is an important part of authentic assessment. Newsletters, home response journals, and videos in which students tell their parents what they've done and learned in school are other ways of assessing and opening communication between home and school.

It is true that extra planning and preparation are involved when teachers move beyond traditional report cards and assessments. But it is well worth the effort. Parents, students, and teachers get more meaningful and in-depth information about what is happening in school, what has been learned, and about goals for future growth.

Problems and Concerns About Alternative Assessment

Giving students choices often goes hand-in-hand with alternative methods of assessment. Make sure Student Choices correspond to the standards you are trying to assess. Some options or topics may yield easier projects than others and cannot be assessed in the same way. As demonstrated and discussed on previous pages, you need to make sure the assessment for each choice is clear before the choices are made. For more information about designing Student Choice activities, see The Planner on page 18 of this book.

Interdisciplinary tasks are often hard to assess and evaluate unless the teacher can distinguish the levels of performance in a variety of content areas. Think through assessment criteria in each content area for each task. For example, if the project is writing and performing a historical monologue, assessment criteria in language arts, history, and performing arts could all be used in assessing this performance.

Performances that result from cooperative group efforts are often harder to assess than the work of individual students. One approach is to include an individual assessment component, though even that is somewhat affected by the group. Self-assessment and peer assessment from group members are also helpful in this situation. And in any group project or performance, the ability to work as a team should be one of the assessment criteria.

Alternative assessment methods are more difficult to use in higher-stakes assessments involving funding, compliance with *NCLB* directives, placement, and scholarships because a higher level of objectivity and equity is needed in such situations. While standardized tests will probably remain the norm in these areas, alternative assessment has the potential to enrich and expand the information that assessment in general can provide.

> **Not everything that counts can be counted and not everything that can be counted counts.**
> Albert Einstein

Alternative/ Authentic/Performance Assessment

Teacher Reflection Page

An environment that encourages alternative or authentic assessment is described below. Assess yourself and your classroom situation to see which of these you are already doing, which you would like to do more, and which you would like to try for the first time.

My Students . . .

_____ 1. do projects on a regular basis, including multiple Student Choice projects in the same content or interest area.

_____ 2. become involved with problems which require an array of knowledge and good judgment about where and how to use that knowledge.

_____ 3. work on problems representative of those found in real life, applying knowledge from a variety of content areas effectively and creatively.

_____ 4. know and understand assessment criteria and standards so that they are able to prepare and self-assess with accuracy.

_____ 5. use formative assessments to evaluate and assess their own work as it progresses and relate it to other work they have done previously.

_____ 6. discuss, share, and learn from each other on a regular basis.

_____ 7. have real audiences for products or performances beyond just doing work as a class requirement.

_____ 8. strive for constant improvement through continually developing higher standards of excellence and working on tasks that require a quality product or performance.

Additional Resources

Three other resources that explore Assessment in more depth are listed and described below. All are published by Pieces of Learning. For more information, log onto www.piecesoflearning.com.

Solving the Assessment Puzzle: Piece by Piece

This book looks at all aspects of assessment, including standards and benchmarks, standardized testing, performance assessment, report cards and grades, complex rubrics, checklists, criteria cards, student-led conferences, and more. It includes 74 ready-to-use rubrics, 40 Criteria Cards, and 6 customizable rubric forms. The book can also be purchased with a CD ROM including all the forms in the book.

Standards-Based Activities and Assessments for the Differentiated Classroom

This user-friendly book has 49 ready-to-use units of work with hundreds of activities and corresponding assessments. Formats for the units include Tic-Tac-Toe, Tiered lessons, and the **Individual Lesson Plan™ (ILP)** like those found throughout this book. Assessment criteria for each activity are listed clearly in a checklist fashion. Also included are 30 criteria cards for commonly used student products. A CD of the entire book is included.

Product Tool Bag

K-1st; 2nd-3rd; and **4th-5th grade CDs** include Product Descriptions, vocabulary, project help, and rubrics for each product. Full-color ready-to-use completely customizable WORD files. K-1st includes 25 products/rubrics; 2nd-3rd includes 34 products/rubrics; and 4th-5th includes 44 products/rubrics.

Reflections

* Standardized test scores are seen as an extremely important indicator of student learning in most school districts, yet there is sometimes a wide gap between what is taught in the classroom and what is assessed by these tests.

* These tests are widely used because they provide data for statewide, national, or international comparisons of student progress and student learning.

* The *NCLB* law has placed a great deal of emphasis and importance on standardized testing.

* Student assessment encompasses much more than test taking.

* Authentic assessment measures assess student performance in context and are alternatives to tests.

* Such assessments generally link directly to classroom instruction and are usually done via observations, criteria cards, rubrics and mini-rubrics.

Chapter 7

Putting It All Together

Questions to Consider

1. What is the relationship between Bloom's Taxonomy, learning modalities, learning styles and Multiple Intelligences?

2. How can I help my students develop higher-level thinking skills, creativity, and research skills as they work on Student Choice activities from the Individual Lesson Plan™ (ILP)?

In the past six chapters, we have investigated the **Individual Lesson Plan™ (ILP)** format and how to use it to incorporate a variety of subject areas, learning styles, learning modalities, or Taxonomy levels. We have discussed Multiple Intelligences and looked at ways to plan classroom activities and lessons for each. We have also examined alternative assessment and ways to establish assessment criteria. While you now have some Tools to use to work with each of these ideas and concepts individually, in "real life" they often work in concert with one another. For example, you may do a learning activity with your students that is at the Application level of Bloom's Taxonomy, is appropriate for a Concrete Random learning style, and uses Visual/Spatial intelligence. We need a way to look at these ideas, synthesizing them so that they can work together.

Look at the **Coil Learning Flowchart™** on the next page. It is a visual representation of how these ideas work together:

We start with the standards. Next we consider Bloom's Taxonomy of Educational Objectives. These define the objectives (aims or goals) for doing the activity.

Students gather information in a Visual, Verbal, Kinesthetic, or Technological mode.

In doing this, they use any combination of the Multiple Intelligences. They also use these as they process the information.

This information is then processed internally through one of the four learning styles.

The result is a Product, Process, and/or Performance, demonstrated via one or more modality.

Finally we define the educational outcomes gained from doing the activity using Bloom's Taxonomy.

Coil Learning Flowchart™

Standards for Learning

Bloom's Taxonomy of Educational Objectives → in Key Subject Areas

Knowledge, Comprehension, Application, Analysis, Synthesis, Evaluation

Gather information through Learning Modalities
Visual, Verbal, Kinesthetic, Technological

Using Multiple Intelligences

Results in . . . .

Product
Process
Performance
Demonstrated through Learning Modalities

Educational Outcomes
Knowledge
Comprehension
Application
Analysis
Synthesis
Evaluation

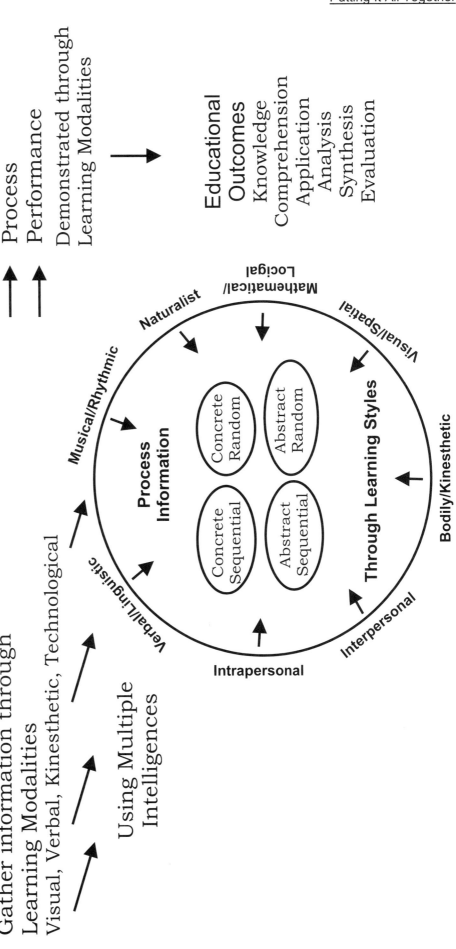

Process Information

Concrete Random

Abstract Random

Concrete Sequential

Abstract Sequential

Naturalist

Mathematical/Logical

Visual/Spatial

Musical/Rhythmic

Verbal/Linguistic

Bodily/Kinesthetic

Through Learning Styles

Interpersonal

Intrapersonal

Writing Questivities™

Using the Questivities™ format is another way to synthesize these ideas. Begin with one of the Student Choice Activities from any of the **Individual Lesson Plans™ (ILPs)** found in this book, or develop your own. Depending upon which format you use, you will already have the Learning Modality, Learning Style, Multiple Intelligences, Subject Area, or Taxonomy level for the activity.

For example, if I use the **Individual Lesson Plan™ (ILP)** on page 53, one of the Student Choice activities listed in the Kinesthetic modality is:

Make an invention from paper and show how it works.

(This is the Project Activity)

I can also identify the following about this activity:

Learning Modality
Kinesthetic

Learning Style
Concrete Random

Taxonomy
Application, Analysis

Multiple Intelligence(s)
Bodily/Kinesthetic
Logical/Mathematical
Visual/Spatial

The next step is to choose assessment criteria. While there are any number of potential criteria for this activity, for this example I have decided upon:

Assessment Mini-Rubric

- Originality/Creativity

- Ability of object to function

- Clear and accurate explanation of what it is and how it works

The **Questivities™** format also includes a *Project Question*. This is a broad question that provides an overall focus for doing the project activity. The **Questivities™** (*Questioning Activities*) **Thinking Questions** are starter questions for students working on the project. They encourage higher-level thinking and creativity by guiding and broadening students' thinking as they brainstorm possible answers. **Questivities**™ promote research skills by taking students beyond just working on the project itself to thinking about it in a broader context. **Questivities**™ **Thinking Questions** are created from a group of phrases which lead to productive questions.

Finally, an ***Active Question*** is included. This activity promotes higher-level thinking skills because in working with an Active Question, students must create a series of their own questions. These, in turn, may create new activities for the thematic unit. An ***Active Question*** is written in the following way:

Make a list of questions _____ might ask _____.

Most of the time the blanks are two inanimate objects. In my example, I have asked that students "Make a list of questions ***a roll of wallpaper*** might ask ***a can of paint***."

Look at the example on the next page to see a completed Questivities.™ format. Page 121 is a reproducible blank form that you can use to write your own Questivities.™

Using Questivities™ as Extensions for Gifted and High-Ability Students

Questivities™ provide a series of higher-level thinking questions that enhance and extend the project activity. Answering these questions results in additional learning, the development of research skills, experience with both divergent and convergent thinking, and offers the opportunity to develop creativity. When all students can do the ILP Student Choice Activities, Questivities™ provide additional opportunities to challenge gifted and talented and other high-ability students.

> **"The test of a first-rate intelligence is the ability to hold two opposing ideas in the mind at the same time and still retain the ability to function."**
>
> **F. Scott Fitzgerald**

Learning Modality

- Kinesthetic

Learning Style

- Concrete Random

Taxonomy Level

- Application, Analysis

Multiple Intelligence

- Bodily/Kinesthetic
- Logical/Mathematical
- Visual/Spatial

Assessment Mini-Rubric

- Originality, Creativity
- Ability of object to function
- Clear and accurate explanation of what it is and how it works

Project Question

- How are new things created or invented?

Inventors & Inventions Questivities™

Project Activity

Make an invention from paper, and explain how it works.

Questivities™ Thinking Questions

1. List all the kinds of paper you could use to make your contraption.
2. Compare/contrast something made from paper with something made from wood.
3. What would happen if everything in your house was made from paper?
4. Would you rather work with paper or work with clay?
5. How would you feel if you could never use any paper at school? What would school be like?
6. Why do people in Japan use paper for so many things, such as origami, windows on homes, noshigami (money envelopes), etc?
7. How could you make your paper contraption look more beautiful?

Active Question

Make a list of questions a roll of wallpaper might ask a can of paint.

Directions: Answer the Questivities™ Thinking Questions and the Active Question before doing the Project Activity.

Learning Modality

• _____

Learning Style

• _____

Taxonomy Level

• _____

• _____

Multiple Intelligence

• _____

Assessment Mini-Rubric

• _____

• _____

• _____

Project Question

• _____

unit title
Questivities™
Project Activity

Questivities™ Thinking Questions

1. List _____

2. Compare/contrast _____

3. What would happen if _____

4. Would you rather _____

5. How would you feel if _____

6. Why _____

7. How _____

Active Question

Make a list of questions _____ might ask _____

Directions: Answer the Questivities™ Thinking Questions and the Active Question before doing the Project Activity.

Reflections

* The **Coil Learning Flowchart**™ is a visual representation of how Bloom's Taxonomy, learning modalities, learning styles and Multiple Intelligences work together.

* Questivities™ provide starter Thinking Questions for students as they work on learning activities and projects. They encourage, stimulate, and promote higher-level thinking skills, creativity, and research skills.

* Questivities™ differentiate **ILP**™ activities for gifted and high-ability students.

Notes

Chapter 8

The Heart of Teaching

Questions to Consider

1. What characteristics make teachers motivational and inspiring to their students?

2. What can I do to make a difference in the lives of my students?

"I have a hard time learning in school," Tamara confided to me. "But I think my teachers like me and I know they are trying to help me. One of my teachers takes time every day to make sure I can catch up on my work."

"Some teachers only care about their subject," complained Wayne. "They don't care at all about me. When I try to explain anything about what's going on in my life or what's bothering me, they don't even want to listen. They just say, 'That's your problem.' Maybe some things are my problem, but you'd think they would try to help. Most teachers are against the students."

These two students present two different views of teachers. Their opinions echo the diverse opinions students have of teachers everywhere. As teachers, we can become proficient in all the new educational theories. We can be technically excellent, effective, and efficient in our teaching. Yet we may never make any difference in the lives of our students. We need something more, that undefinable emotional element that makes teaching an art, not a science. It is the most important teaching tool of all. I like to call it the "HeART of Teaching."

I often ask my workshop audiences to remember **"The Teacher"** in their lives, that one very special teacher who inspired and motivated them above all others. I find that in an audience of teachers, nearly 90% have had that one special teacher touch their lives in a very profound way. For many, this one special teacher is THE REASON they decided to become teachers.

This was certainly my experience. I was fortunate to have many good, even excellent, teachers during my school years. But there was one who motivated and inspired me, who "touched my heart" in a very special way with her caring and her love, and had such an impact on my life that even today I would say she is one of the major influences in making me the person I am. This special teacher is Mrs. Mary C. Walker, who was my teacher in junior high school.

When I was in junior high, I thought long and hard about the meaning of teaching and what being a good teacher was really all about. I wrote these thoughts to my special teacher and gave them to her the last day of school. Many years went by. Recently Mrs. Walker retired and sent my paper, now yellowed with age, back to me. I had totally forgotten about writing it, but she had kept it all these years! As I read it I realized I still feel essentially the same about the true meaning of teaching. On the next page are the words I wrote and a picture of Mrs. Walker and me taken many years ago.

A Good Teacher

A good teacher likes to teach, likes what she teaches, and loves those she teaches.

A good teacher sees each child as an important person, not as a 'thing' for psychiatric analysis or a 'thing' that must be taught.

A good teacher sees herself as an instrument of God – one who is learning through her children rather than the one who knows everything and must teach it to someone who doesn't know as much as she does.

A good teacher finds enjoyment in merely being with her children, sharing their joys and woes and sharing with them a relationship in which learning goes not only from her to them, but from them to her, too.

Carolyn Coil   Age 13

Mrs. Walker

Psychiatrist Dr. Robert Coles suggests that teachers can reach the hearts of their students by sharing their own stories, memories, passions, and interests. Students might say teachers like that are "real" and caring.

Schools must deal with both the head and the heart. If we reach the hearts of our students, we can then awaken their minds. Students who receive insufficient positive attention from peers and adults in school will either fade into the woodwork so that they become essentially invisible, or they will act out and get attention even by negative means. These students are truly "at risk." It is only a matter of time before they will drop out mentally and probably physically as well.

The greatest need of all students is to know we value and love them. Students need to recognize that teachers care about them as individuals. Successful, high achieving students usually feel this way, but other students often do not. What can we do about that? We can take a genuine interest in all of our students, really caring about each of them. Each of us can be a teacher with heART!

Movies and Videos
That Show the Heart of Teaching

Conrack
Dangerous Minds   Dead Poets Society
Emperor's Club   Fame
Finding Forrester   Good Will Hunting
Kindergarten Cop   Lean on Me
Man Without a Face   Music of the Heart
Mr. Holland's Opus   Remember the Titans
Stand and Deliver   Wonder Boys

For a list of additional movies visit:
http://www.mbteach.org/teachermovies/100movies.htm

> **"There will be no freedom without intelligence, And no real intelligence without heart."**
>
> **Luis Machado**

Reflections

* Teaching is more than proficiency and efficiency in teaching the standards and implementing educational standards and techniques. There is an emotional element in teaching that I call the heART of teaching.

* Students must know that we truly care about them, that we value and love them, and that we have a genuine interest in their lives.

The HEART of Teaching

Teacher Reflection Page

Share your thoughts about the heart of teaching with at least one of your colleagues.

Think about your school days. Who was your favorite teacher? What were the things you particularly liked about him or her?

What affective or emotional characteristics make a good teacher? What personal characteristics do students respond to?

What personal characteristics do you have that make you a good teacher? How can you enhance these?

What personal characteristics do you have that detract from your effectiveness as a teacher? How can you minimize them?

How have your views on teaching changed since your school days? Which have remained essentially the same?

What emotional and personal needs do your students have? With which of these needs do you feel most able to help?

Chapter 9

Cultural & Linguistic Diversity

Questions to Consider

1. In what ways is cultural diversity a strength? In what ways is it a challenge?

2. What terminology do we use when talking about cultural & linguistic diversity?

3. What teaching strategies should I use with English Language Learners?

4. How are learning styles and cultural diversity interrelated?

5. Why should we include multicultural themes and concepts in our curriculum units?

My mother's parents were both first generation German-American, as their parents emigrated to America from Germany in the late 1800s and subsequently had children who met and married. My father's mother was of English descent and his father was Dutch. When I was a child, I used to proudly declare, "I am an English/Dutch/German American!" I am married to a man whose father had Irish roots and whose maternal grandparents came from Scotland. Our children, then, are Scotch/ Irish/English/Dutch/German Americans! Each family has its own saga of diversity. The stories and histories of America's families are witnesses to the cultural diversity that is everywhere in our country.

Cultural diversity is one of the great strengths of our country. We have always been a nation of many cultures and national origins. Our stores and restaurants have products and foods from all over the world; our music, visual and performing arts, and popular culture contain a rich variation of ethnic offerings; our styles and fashions have a multitude of origins.

Our diversity, however, also presents one of the biggest challenges for 21st century teachers. Cultural and ethnic differences can result in misunderstandings, conflict, and violence. Teaching students from a variety of cultural and linguistic backgrounds can be difficult at best. Historically, different ethnic groups have been separate from one another, but this is rapidly changing. A mix of student populations is now found in city, suburban, small town, and rural schools. It has become increasingly important to include everyone, to have enough resources to go around, and to ensure equity without sacrificing excellence.

Consider these facts:

- Students from non-English speaking backgrounds are the fastest growing group of students in our schools.

- In the 2003-2004 school year, 5.5 million students in American schools were learning English as their second language.

- There was a 100% increase in English language learners from 1994-2004 but only a 10% increase in other students.

- The 2000 Census documents more than 300 different languages spoken in the United States.

- By 2050, the Latino population of the United States is projected to be 24% of the entire population.

- Asian Americans are projected to be 10% of the U.S. population by 2050.

- The fastest growing ethnic group in the United States is of Hispanic origin.
  (U.S. Population Project www.pade.msu.edu/data/uspopproject1996_2005.html)

New Non-English Speaking Immigrants

Recent demographic changes present us with new challenges in the 21st century. The United States is a nation of increasing ethnic, linguistic, and cultural diversity. This trend is affecting schools across America, from urban areas to the traditionally more homogeneous suburbs and small towns. Although the total number of children in our country has increased by only 10% since the 1980s, the racial and ethnic composition of school-age children changed dramatically. According to the most recent population projections, this trend toward greater and greater cultural diversity will continue at least until the mid 21st century.

With an influx of new non-English speaking immigrants in many schools, teachers may face many students who do not speak English well enough to follow the standard curriculum. What tools can we use to best assimilate and teach these students?

Approaches to English Language Learning

There are a number of approaches to teaching students who are learning English. Some favor English immersion and English-only instruction. They believe this approach is more inclusive and helps assimilate immigrant students more quickly. Others claim that bilingual programs are better because students learn literacy skills and content knowledge in their native language while they are learning English.

A summary of the most common approaches is below:

- Bilingual programs: Emphasize both maintaining the student's native language and developing English language skills. Content is taught in the student's native language.

- Dual Immersion: This approach is usually offered in a magnet school setting. Approximately half of the children in the class are native English speakers and half are native speakers of one other language. In general, half of the instruction is in English and half is in the other language. The goal of the program is for all children to develop fluency in both languages.

- ESL pullout: Supplements the mainstream classroom with small group instruction during a portion of the school day. The focus of the instruction is on developing English language skills.

- Sink-or-swim approach: Regular classroom instruction with no special help.

- Structured immersion: Instruction is almost totally in English but is done in a self-contained classroom where all of the children are English language learners.

No Child Left Behind (NCLB) and English Language Learners

No Child Left Behind (NCLB) requires English language learners, like all other subgroups, to take high stakes tests. Most schools and school districts show a large test score and achievement gap between these students and others at their same age and grade level.

One reason for this gap is that even when ELLs (English Language Learners) have learned basic language skills and are fluent in social situations, they are generally not well-versed in academic English. However, from upper elementary grades on, this is the English they need to know to do well on tests and to succeed in school. One strategy for closing the achievement gap is to be intentional about teaching Academic English to these students.

Academic English:

1) Describes content and subject area knowledge

2) Includes the specific vocabulary of the subject

3) Expresses thinking concepts and processes students need to do while interacting with the content

Understanding the Terminology of Cultural and Linguistic Diversity

A number of different terms are used when discussing culturally and/or linguistically diverse students. Some of the most common terms are below. For a complete glossary, log onto: www.helpforschools.com/ELLKBase/glossary.shtml

- **Bi-cultural:** Identifying with the cultures of two different language or ethnic groups

- **Bilingual:** Skilled to some degree in two languages; for example, someone who speaks both English and Spanish

- **ELL(s):** Refers to *English Language Learner(s)*. These students are in the process of learning English. Therefore, they have a degree of difficulty comprehending, speaking, reading, and/or writing English. This affects their school performance in English.

- **ENL:** Refers to *English as a New Language*. These students are just beginning to learn English.

- **ESL:** Means *English as a Second Language* and refers to classes, techniques, and/or a special curriculum offered to ELL students.

- **ESOL:** Means *English to Speakers of Other Languages*. This acronym is sometimes used interchangeably with ESL.

- **LEP:** Means *Limited English Proficiency*. An LEP student is not fully English proficient, speaks a language other than English at home, and does not fully demonstrate English language skills in comprehension, speaking, reading, and/or writing. This terminology is used in the Federal law.

Cultural Differences in Students

Language development is not the only concern in teaching immigrant students. Cultural differences and adjustments are equally important. Many of these students even at age 12 or 13 have never been to school. Because they are not familiar with the American way of life, many immigrant students and their parents are not familiar with the structure and culture of schooling. They do not understand such things as how to enroll in school or even how the school calendar works.

Immigrant students cannot be thought of as one group. In fact, they are amazingly diverse. They have diverse differences in background, experiences, education, and motivation. Some are very literate in their native language while others are not. Some have had rich educational experiences while others have never attended school. Some have lots of family support while others have little or none at all. Some already speak English while others do not. Some speak Latin-based languages with similarities to English while others speak languages with no roots in Latin. Some come from cultures with similarities to American culture while others find American culture completely different and strange.

This chapter looks at both linguistic and cultural differences and how we can work with both in schools.

Principles of Second Language Development

There are several basic principles of Second Language Development. Read and think about these carefully. Then discuss them with a colleague.

1. Students need to feel at ease with themselves and positive about their relationships with others in new language situations.

2. Comprehension comes before language is spoken or written. Therefore, students will understand what is being said before they can express themselves well.

3. Competency in speaking a new language develops more quickly when students are focused on doing things while using the new language in a natural way rather than focusing on the language itself.

4. Students can learn to read and write in a new language at the same time they are developing oral skills.

5. Everyone learns a new language through a lot of repetition and through trial and error. Learning from mistakes is part of the learning process.

What are the implications of the above for teaching students who are learning English?

Using the Push-in Unit Planner

One helpful approach in working with students who are learning English is to be intentional about planning for their needs when they are in a regular classroom setting. The **Push-in Planner** found on the next two pages is a visual organizer to guide your thinking as you plan.

Push-In Unit Planner

Title of Unit _____

Grade/Subject _____ Time frame for Unit _____

List main topics in this unit.

What standards will be covered in this unit?

What questions should students be able to answer after completing this unit?

What aspects of English do students need to know to complete the classroom tasks for this unit?
(Example: Take notes, compare/contrast, present orally)

What are the major terms or academic/technical vocabulary students need to know in this unit?

What are the major assignments in this unit? Can any be modified for LEP students?

What background knowledge in the topic should students have to learn successfully in this unit?

List resources (books, web sites, magazines, videos, etc.) that will help students learn the information in this unit.

How can LEP students be encouraged to join class discussion during this unit?

How will learning be assessed for this unit? Can any assessments be modified for LEP students?

30 Strategies for Working with LEP/ESL Students

1. Use the "chalk story" method when you tell a story or share an idea, making drawings as you talk.

2. Share personal stories and include artifacts or photos.

3. Use body movements, facial expressions, gestures, hand motions, and other non-verbals that get the message across.

4. Use manipulatives and concrete methods of teaching.

5. Give directions in more than one way. Keep them simple. Repeat when necessary.

6. Talk at a slower pace, and use shorter sentences.

7. Avoid idioms and slang expressions.

8. Adapt materials to make the language more simple, but do not "water down" the content.

9. Present work in smaller amounts. Give LEP/ESL students who are struggling academically smaller increments of work at a time. This helps the student who is overwhelmed by a large assignment.

10. Reduce the amount of reading and writing an LEP/ESL student is required to do. Ask yourself, *"What are the essentials in this assignment?"* Adapt the amount of work required depending on the pace the student is able to set for the task at hand.

11. Provide extra time to complete assignments.

12. Give students a copy of class notes with the major points listed that will be covered in class discussion.

13. If the student has trouble copying items from the board, have the assignment written out for him/her ahead of time and include pictures or graphics to help with comprehension.

14. Make sure each student has a looseleaf notebook or folder so that all of his or her papers can be kept in one place. This is a new concept for some LEP/ESL students who have little or no experience attending school.

15. Mark pages that need to be done with a paper clip or Post-it®-note.

16. Allow the student to underline or circle answers instead of writing them. Encourage the use of highlighters and other writing tools.

17. Make the format of written assignments easy to read and understand. Give forms with lots of white space and places to write information. Don't give too much information on one page.

18. Use lots of visuals, demonstrations, and hands-on learning when teaching significant concepts. Pictures, illustrations, diagrams, charts, graphs, maps, etc. will help convey your message visually and help students in identifying concepts and seeing relationships.

19. Use a variety of graphic organizers such as T-Charts, concept maps, flowcharts, K-W-L charts, outlines, and other visual organizers that can be used by students to help direct their thinking.

20. Use story mapping to help students sequence events in a story or novel. Supply crayons or markers along with large sheets of paper (chart paper or newsprint) and ask students to draw pictures or images to show events in the story along with text. This is an excellent group activity and helps all students to better understand the story.

21. Have the students create "shape stories," writing one-page stories or small books on paper cut into the shape of an object relating to the topic.

22. Show students examples of good projects or good work before they begin.

23. Create and use flash cards with words on the front and pictures on the back, or for older students, two or three cards showing the same concept both visually and verbally.

24. Use various strategies for group work such as Think-Pair-Share, Jigsaws, Cooperative Learning, etc.

25. Have lots of opportunities for LEP/ESL students to practice talking in low-stress, informal situations.

26. State items in a positive manner when correcting oral language. Use phrases such as *"Let's say"* instead of *"Don't say it that way!"*

27. Use the **Push-In Planner** on pages 131-132 to identify main concepts, ideas, vocabulary, and questions students should know at the end of a unit of study.

28. Teach integrated, thematic units in which students have choices of activities for learning, especially those based on learning modalities or multiple intelligences. See the **Individual Lesson Plan™ (ILP)** format and sample units in this book.

29. Identify the academic English students need to know to successfully complete assignments. Support them in learning academic terms and concepts.

30. Use technological tools to support learning.

- Use tape recorders for storytelling, data collection, and oral journals.

- Encourage the use of word processors and graphics programs.

- Use photos and digital cameras to help students communicate.

- Use technological tools for multimedia projects.

- Encourage online research.

- Have students share with one another via e-mail and online courses.

- Teach organizational skills by having students keep a visual organizer of the web sites they have visited.

- Find software that will reinforce needed skills.

- Use computer adaptive testing with tests automatically tailored to the appropriate language level.

Cultural Diversity and Learning Styles

Culture affects learning style and learning modality preferences. To help culturally diverse students achieve, teachers need to use a variety of teaching styles consistent with their students' learning styles. The lesson planning formats found in the first part of this book will be helpful tools in structuring classroom activities that meet the needs of 21st century students from diverse cultural backgrounds.

Students from different cultures do learn differently. There are some valid generalizations about differences in learning style from culture to culture, though individual students within each cultural group may differ from one another.

Students from African American and Hispanic cultures generally prefer learning to take place holistically rather than in small separate parts. Students from these cultures may have difficulty in classrooms where knowledge is broken into parts rather than looked at as a whole. They also tend to be field sensitive learners. This means that the social and personal climate of the classroom is important to their learning and that they learn best when they have a personal relationship with the teacher and can interact with their peers.

Students from Asian and Western European (Anglo) backgrounds come from cultures that emphasize field independent learning; that is, learning independently and not involving emotions in the learning situation. This type of student may love doing independent study with little teacher guidance or peer interaction.

Cultural backgrounds can also affect student learning and school functioning. Consider the implications of the following generalizations:

- Hispanic students come from cultures where families value unity and interdependence within the extended family and where the family highly respects traditions. This culture has a flexible sense of time and uses physical closeness and emotional intensity during conversation.

- Asian American students also have strong extended family connections and an orientation toward tradition. Their culture respects authority and structure and values silence and privacy. They have a preference for modesty, reserve, and self-control and a hesitancy about spontaneity and creative thinking.

- African American students have strong "in group" values, a group world view, and prefer a call/response style of communication. Their culture shows emotional intensity and expression in oral communication and they prefer spontaneity, physical expression, and creative thinking.

- Students from Western European (Anglo American) cultural backgrounds come from cultures that value individualism, competitiveness, and the nuclear rather than the extended family. They prefer order, control, and logic rather than emotion and spontaneity in responses and decision making.

"America is not like a blanket – one piece of unbroken cloth, the same color, the same texture, the same size. America is more like a quilt – many pieces, many colors, many sizes, all woven and held together by a common thread" - Jesse Jackson

Cultural Diversity

Teacher Reflection Page

1. Trace your own ethnic and cultural roots. List some cultural characteristics that you possess from each group. (For example, family traditions, music, food, memorabilia, etc.)

2. America has been called "A Nation of Immigrants" and "A Melting Pot." Jesse Jackson has labeled us a patchwork quilt. Think of a metaphor that most aptly describes your class or your school. Invite your students to brainstorm with you.

3. List the cultural and ethnic groups represented by your students. You may be surprised at how many of your students come from a variety of cultural backgrounds. Look at the cultural characteristics discussed on page 135. Which characteristics best describe which students?

Student(s)	Cultural Characteristic

4. What is your biggest problem or concern in working with a culturally diverse group of students? Write your problem in the space below. Find strategies to help solve this problem as you read the remainder of this chapter.

Rating Scale for Success
in a Culturally Diverse Learning Environment

The conditions and attitudes listed below are important in creating an optimum learning environment for a culturally diverse group of students. Think about your own school and/or classroom situation. Then use the Rating Scale below to see how well your school is equipped to meet the needs of culturally diverse learners.

1 = Do not have this at all   2 = Seldom   3 = Sometimes   4 = Often   5 = Always

_____ 1. Equal opportunities for all students to learn

_____ 2. Cultural awareness among students, parents, educators & support staff.

_____ 3. Opportunities for community interaction with the school where people from a mix of cultural backgrounds are involved

_____ 4. Uncrowded classrooms where individual needs can be met

_____ 5. Qualified educators with an openness to cultural diversity

_____ 6. Appropriate enrichment materials that reflect a variety of cultures

_____ 7. Social relationships among peers, educators, and support staff.

_____ 8. Shared decision-making both in individual classrooms and throughout the school

_____ 9. Multicultural curriculum and instruction

_____ 10. Opportunities to develop problem solving, cooperative, and interpersonal skills

Scoring

50 - 41   You are in a school where students from all cultures should do very well.

40 - 31   Your school has many attributes for success with cultural diversity.

30 - 21   You have some positive elements in working with culturally diverse students, but there is room for improvement.

20 - 11   Your school needs to make the needs of cultural diverse students a top priority.

10 - 0   Your school needs to examine ways to meet the needs of all students, and then make a plan for implementation.

Strategies for Working with Culturally Diverse Students

Teachers should know the essential elements of their students' cultural backgrounds and know how to interpret their students' behavior from a cultural perspective. Below are some specific strategies that will help you to work with culturally diverse students.

1. Talk with your students to find out more about their culture.

2. Respect the cultural knowledge of your students; become a learner of their cultural ideas!

3. Consult a school counselor or ESL specialist in your school district to learn more about the various cultures of your students.

4. Encourage students to write about their experiences and the places they have lived.

5. Use advisory committees with members who represent a variety of cultures.

6. Develop partnerships with local businesses who are successful in serving people from a variety of cultures.

7. During discussion times, use terminology and ideas from a variety of cultures.

8. Help students new to your school and/or new to this country understand how school works. Things we take for granted such as how to go through the lunch line, what a bell means, or what books and materials should be taken to class may be a mystery to students from other cultures.

9. Assess each child's strengths as well as his or her weaknesses. *

10. Modify thematic units, classroom materials, and activities to include a variety of cultures.

11. Create a positive and welcoming classroom climate that invites sharing and communication among all students.

12. Have culturally diverse magazines, books, newspapers, etc. available as classroom resources.

13. Take advantage of workshops, seminars, university courses, international organizations, tours and exchange programs, and one-on-one conversations with people from different cultures to increase your own cultural awareness.

14. Use poetry as a vehicle for expressing cultural experiences. On the next page is an example of this in a poem written by a 5th grader who is a recent immigrant.

* (See pages 99-102 and *Motivating Underachievers* and *Becoming an Achiever* by Carolyn Coil for useful assessment tools.)

"Feelings"

Playing with my friends,
> Mom calls.

I'm going to the United States,
> Feeling happy.

Going to the airport,
> Feeling nervous.

Traveling to the United States,
> Feeling excited.

I was not going to see my family,
> Feeling sad.

Traveling in a car, Seeing my dad,
> Feeling great.

Going to Jackson School,
> Feeling scared.

Meeting new people, Seeing some faces I know,
> Feeling happy again.

Three years later,
> Feeling good because it feels like home.

Carol Dominquez, Grade 5

Jackson School, Seymour, Indiana

Strategies for Working with Culturally Diverse Families

Knowing about the cultural background of the families of your students is extremely important, especially in a school that includes several different cultures. Below are some strategies to consider as you work with the families of your students.

1. Invite parents to visit the school before their child is enrolled. Try to make them feel at home in the school setting.

2. Be sure to listen carefully to parents to develop an understanding of their values and beliefs.

3. Invite parents to participate in school programs in any way it is convenient to their individual schedules.

4. Talk to parents about volunteering in school and sharing information and customs about their culture with all students. Do this on a small scale at first so you don't frighten them!

5. Identify all of the significant adults for the child within the family structure. This is particularly important in cultures with large extended families.

6. Encourage parents to bring an interpreter to conferences and/or try to locate interpreters for parents who do not speak English.

7. Have an all-school talent show or other event where parents can see their children working in partnership with children of other cultures.

8. Make phone calls or have conferences with parents explaining school procedures in areas such as report cards, testing, or other means of assessment, school awards, school programs, etc. Parents may be totally unaware of many of these procedures.

9. Plan and implement school-wide classroom ethnic-oriented social events. Enlist parent help.

10. Make print materials available to parents in their native language. Web sites such as www.freetranslation.com are useful in translating materials. For Spanish speaking parents, see *Practical Tips for Parents*, reproducible newsletters for parents written in Spanish and English published by Pieces of Learning.

Multicultural Teaching

"Multicultural education is simply teaching people about other cultures, starting with the cultures they encounter every day. We want students to know about the cultures surrounding them and the cultures they may encounter later in life." – Bruce Davis, Elementary School Principal, Rosemead, California

Most educators realize that all students need to learn not only about their own culture but also about the cultures of others; for they either live at present – or in the future will live – in a multicultural environment. Schools need to teach not only about various cultures around the world, but also about the various cultures within our own country and our own communities.

Curriculum is continuing to expand to include the cultures of the many diverse groups that make up the United States. For the most part, multicultural education has been included in the content areas of social studies, history, and literature, and in interdisciplinary thematic units. As teachers who are preparing students for living throughout most of the 21st century, you need to develop proficiency in designing lessons from a multicultural perspective, thereby teaching your students about other cultures in the world. The challenge is to create an environment that is respectful of different cultures, but at the same time, maintain a common culture within your school or classroom with which everyone can identify.

Thematic units are tools that work well in teaching students concepts and key ideas such as immigration, language, intercultural relations, holidays and celebrations, myths and folk tales, conflict, etc. Use different activities related to a specific theme to help your students see a variety of perspectives. For example, have them participate in role playing, with various students showing differing perspectives through the roles they have taken on. This will help your students become critical thinkers as they see different sides to an issue or question.

A Multicultural Unit Using the ILP™ Format

On the next page, you will see a planning web for a thematic unit entitled "We Are Multicultural" that can be used to increase multicultural understanding. Page 143 shows how the **Individual Lesson Plan™ (ILP)** format can be used to give Students Choices in the learning activities based on this theme. A sample of Questivities™ (page 144) shows how to extend your students' multicultural understanding. On page 145 there is a Visual Organizer for Compare/Contrast activities. It shows how this form was used by students to compare and contrast three ethnic groups. Use the blank form on page 146 to work with your students. You may wish to adapt or modify either form to better suit the specific needs and/or cultural origins of your students.

We Are Multicultural

Make a chart comparing and contrasting at three cultures represented by students in your class.

Demonstrate/explain a sport, dance, or cultural event from another country.

Take a survey of ethnic foods people eat. Generate a graph showing results.

Make a list of at least 25 English words that come from other languages. Explain why they are part of the English language.

Make a list of questions you have about another country. Post on a computer bulletin board. Record the answers you receive.

Research 3 web sites that tell about everyday life in another country. Generate a visual summarizing your findings.

Summarize a folktale from another culture for your class. Dress in costume.

Wear the native costume of another culture. Explain its meaning and function.

Make a list of holidays from a variety of cultures. Make an illustrated encyclopedia of these holidays.

Make a 3-D poster showing what people from a variety of cultures think is "beautiful."

Make a large world map labeling the ethnic and cultural origins of the students in your class.

Role play some problems a non-English speaking student might have at your school.

INDIVIDUAL LESSON PLAN - We Are Multicultural

ACTIVITIES - STUDENT CHOICES

Visual

1. Make a list of holidays from a variety of cultures. Make an illustrated encyclopedia of these holidays.
2. Make a large world map labeling the ethnic/cultural origins of the student sin your class.
3. Make a chart comparing and contrasting three cultures represented by students in your class. (see page 145-146)

Verbal

7. Share a folktale from another culture with your class. Dress in costume.
8. Role play some problems a non-English speaking student might have at your school.
9. Make a list of at least 25 English words that come from other languages. Explain why they are part of the English language.

Kinesthetic

4. Make a poster showing what people from a variety of cultures think is "beautiful."
5. Wear the native costume of another culture. Explain its meaning & function.
6. Demonstrate/explain a sport, dance, or cultural event from another country.

Technological

10. Survey ethnic foods people eat. Generate a graph showing results.
11. Make a list of questions you have about another country. Post on a computer bulletin board. Record the answers.
12. Research 3 web sites that tell about everyday life in another country. Generate a visual summarizing your findings.

Required Activities Teacher's Choice

1. Make a family tree showing your family's origins.
2. On a world map, identify and color code the countries of your ancestors' origins.
3. Read a book that is set in another culture or one about a person from another culture. Summarize the book in a short illustrated report.

Product/Performance Required

1. Family Tree
2. Map
3. Illustrated report

Assessment Required Activities

1. Accurate visual Visually pleasing
2. Accurate labeling of countries
3. Report reflects cultural differences Illustration compliments written report

Optional Student-Parent Cooperative Activity Interview a relative or family friend from another culture. Use an audio or video tape to record your interview.

Student Choices in Ways to Learn

Visual

_____

Verbal

_____

Kinesthetic

_____

Technological

_____

Product/Performance Student Choice

Standards

Due Date Student Choice

Learning Modality

- Visual

Learning Style

- Concrete Sequential

Taxonomy Level

- Knowledge, Comprehension

Multiple Intelligence

- Interpersonal
- Visual/Spatial

Assessment Mini-Rubric

- Includes all students
- Accurate geographically
- Neatly done

Project Question

- What are the ethnic/cultural origins of the students in your class?

We Are Multicultural

Questivities™
Project Activity

Make a large map and label the ethnic/cultural origins of all the students in your class.

Questivities™ Thinking Questions

1. List all the students in your class and at least one ethnic/cultural group for each.
2. Compare/contrast characteristics of two different ethnic/cultural groups.
3. What would happen if everyone in your school came from just one culture?
4. Would you rather be friends with people just like you or with people different from you? Why?
5. How would you feel if you were told your ethnic/cultural group was totally bad? totally perfect?
6. Why do some people dislike people who are different from them?
7. How can you help classmates avoid prejudice?

Active Question

Make a list of questions a new immigrant might ask the Statue of Liberty.

Directions: Answer the Questivities™ Thinking Questions and the Active Question before doing the Project Activity.

A Visual Organizer for Compare/Contrast Activities

Ethnic Groups in Our Class

Below are topics to consider when comparing and contrasting each group. Some information has been filled in for each item. Your students may be able to add more. Have students continue to list similarities and differences.

When did this group come to America?

Asian-American	African American	Native American
Chinese immigrants 1850 Japanese immigrants 1900 Southeast Asian immigrants 1973-1990s	Through the slave trade from the early 1700s to 1865	From Asia over Bering Strait land bridge 20,000 years ago

What are some important contributions?

Asian-American	African American	Native American
Completion of railroad east to west Engineering, math, science	Fight for civil rights and desegregation Sports, music, literature, politics	Foods such as corn and squash Love of the environment and the land Survival skills

Instances of unfair treatment

Asian-American	African American	Native American
Internment of Japanese during WWII	Slavery Discrimination Segregation in schools and housing	Land taken away Cherokee Trail of Tears Treaties broken

A Visual Organizer for Compare/Contrast Activities

When students are asked to do a Compare/Contrast activity, this visual organizer should help them to more easily see similarities and differences. First, brainstorm questions or topics that could be considered in comparing and contrasting. Write each on the appropriate line on the visual organizer. Then fill in the information for each item. From this students will be able to list similarities and differences.

Question or topic

Item 1	Item 2	Item 3

Question or topic

Item 1	Item 2	Item 3

Question or topic

Item 1	Item 2	Item 3

Some Final Thoughts About Multicultural Education

Multicultural education should not divide students. Instead it should be a tool to use in uniting your students who come from such diverse backgrounds. The goal is to create authentic unity that reflects an understanding of all your students' experiences. Begin by examining differences, but emphasize what we all have in common. Schools must show both our country's unity and its diversity.

It is not necessary to put an emphasis on victimization or how a minority culture has been victimized by the majority culture. At the same time, you don't avoid controversial issues within a culture such as racism, prejudice, and inequality. Seek to create a realistic balance considering the age of the children you teach.

Young children especially need to see the positive accomplishments of people from a variety of cultures. Avoid stereotypes. Instead describe some global characteristics of various ethnic groups. Be mindful of the fine line between generalizing and stereotyping. Generalizations are necessary for the study of groups because they give us clues about what individuals are like and how and why they act as they do. Stereotypes give absolute answers or negative impressions with few facts or examples to support them. They also cause us to view everyone in a particular group in the same way.

There is no doubt that education can lead to a discussion of issues that can be divisive and cause conflict. Here are guidelines to follow when an area of conflict arises:

Guidelines for Managing Multicultural Discussions and Conflicts

1. Set parameters for the discussion before it begins.

2. Keep the discussion factual not emotional.

3. Help the class work through a conflict or misunderstanding by discussing it rationally.

4. Be a good listener and moderator for the discussion.

5. Be clear that everything presented about various cultures does not have to be tolerated or valued on a personal level.

6. Do not allow the discussion to evolve into name calling.

7. Remind your students that understanding begins with listening to another's point of view.

8. Limit the time to be spent in discussion of a particular issue before the discussion begins.

For further information about conflict management, see Chapter 12.

Reflections

* The cultural diversity of our students is, paradoxically, one of our greatest strengths while it provides one of the greatest challenges for 21st century teachers.

* Terminology to describe cultural and linguistic diversity varies greatly. We need to understand and use these terms correctly.

* There are many excellent teaching strategies to use successfully with English Language Learners. Start with the Principles of Second Language Development, and build from there.

* Valid generalizations can be made about the learning style preferences of each cultural group. However, avoid stereotyping. Individual students within each cultural group can and do differ from one another.

* Students living in a multicultural environment need to explore lessons with multicultural themes to learn multicultural concepts and to learn about the cultures represented by their classmates and neighbors.

Differences in language and culture can cause conflict between the home and the school.
—Baca and Cervantes

Chapter 10

Inclusion of Students With Disabilities

Questions to Consider

1. How have federal laws impacted the education of children with disabilities?

2. What beliefs support the idea of inclusion?

3. Why is inclusion becoming more and more commonplace in American schools?

4. How does inclusion work successfully?

5. What problems and concerns are there about the inclusion process?

Bart is an emotionally disturbed fifth grader. His achievement test scores in both reading and math are below grade level. Yet he often displays lots of intelligence when he writes science fiction stories and draws cartoon illustrations to match. His plots and characters are well developed and show a great deal of creativity, though his grammar and spelling need improvement. Because the regular education teacher works collaboratively with the special education teacher, Bart receives the assistance he needs to keep his behavior under control. Bart can function well included in a regular classroom setting.

Janine has a learning disability. She is in eighth grade but has difficulty in reading and with organizational skills. She is easily distracted and has characteristics of ADD, though she has never been formally diagnosed as having it. Janine is in a middle school committed to the philosophy of inclusion. The special education teacher is one of five teachers on the middle school team. She works with the four subject area teachers in planning curriculum, teaching strategies and lessons, adapting and modifying materials, and working with groups of students who need special help. Janine, along with several other of her disabled and non-disabled classmates, meets with the special ed teacher for a study skills seminar twice a week. Occasionally, Janine also has a time scheduled for some individual tutoring.

Due to an educational practice known as *inclusion*, Bart and Janine, though identified as students with disabilities, are receiving their education in the regular classroom setting. Inclusion is an educational philosophy based on the belief that entitles all students to participate fully in their school community. The term usually refers to the commitment to educate each child, to the maximum extent appropriate, in the school and classroom the student would attend if the disabling condition were not present.

Inclusion has come about due to the belief that children with disabilities who are segregated into special education classrooms are receiving education that is inherently unequal. Many children who have been in special education programs have not developed necessary academic, vocational, or social skills. Inclusion moves such students, along with support services, into the regular classroom.

The inclusion of students with disabilities into the regular classroom has become increasingly common throughout the United States. Federal laws require that schools make a significant effort to find an inclusive setting for the delivery of educational services to students with disabilities. *NCLB's* provisions require most students with disabilities to take the same tests as all other students. This, too, has lead to more inclusion.

Laws Affecting Students with Disabilities

The Individuals with Disabilities Education Improvement Act (IDEA) 2004 states: "Unless a handicapped child's individualized education program requires some other arrangement, the child is educated in the school which he or she would attend if not handicapped." This law also requires states to set goals and standards for special education students that are consistent, to the maximum extent possible, with those for all students. **Section 504 of the Rehabilitation Act of 1973 and amended 1998**, requires: "A recipient of federal funds . . . shall educate, or shall provide for the education of, each qualified handicapped person in its jurisdiction with persons who are not handicapped to the maximum extent appropriate to the needs of the handicapped person."

In the past few years, federal court cases have interpreted these laws to require the inclusion of children with disabilities, even severe disabilities, in the school and classroom they would attend if they were not disabled. Even if they cannot keep up with the academic work, the courts have decided these students must be included if there is a potential social benefit.

The inclusion model involves a disabled child being placed in a regular classroom to the maximum extent appropriate. The aim of inclusion is to integrate the students, along with the supports they need, into classrooms with non-disabled peers. It involves bringing the support services to the child and requires that the child will benefit from this placement in some way (academically, socially, and/or emotionally).

The most common support services are consultation and training for the regular classroom teacher. In schools where inclusion works well, the regular classroom teacher has continual access to and communication with support staff who can help find equipment and materials and help modify teaching techniques to meet the needs of disabled students. Necessary supports in terms of equipment and trained personnel are also necessary for the related medical services needed by some disabled children.

No Child Left Behind (NCLB) and Special Education Students

As of this writing, *NCLB* mandates that students with disabilities perform at the same proficiency level on grade-level standardized tests as other students. Under the provisions of *NCLB*, states must test at least 95% of their students with disabilities. The test scores of these students must be incorporated into school ratings and report cards. The goal is to have all students, including students with disabilities, performing at the proficient level by 2013-2014. Schools are required to make adequate yearly progress (AYP) toward that goal or face sanctions that become progressively more severe.

The U. S. Department of Education is beginning to allow more flexibility under *NCLB* in assessments for special education students. **One percent** of students with **severe cognitive disabilities** can be counted as proficient even if they take alternate assessments that are below grade level. An additional **two percent** of students with **persistent academic disabilities** can be tested using modified assessments. These are students who, even with the best instruction, still cannot meet grade-level standards.

In order to receive these flexible provisions, states must:

- Test at least 95% of their students with disabilities

- Make appropriate accommodations for students with disabilities

- Have alternative assessments in language arts and math for those students with disabilities who are unable to take the regular tests even with accommodations

The result of these more flexible provisions is that states may have a three-tiered system for accountability:

1. Alternate assessments for students with severe cognitive disabilities

2. Modified assessments for students with persistent academic disabilities

3. Standardized regular testing for the remainder of the students

Another consideration is the size a subgroup. The law says each subgroup (such as children with disabilities or low-income children) must make adequate yearly progress (AYP), but the states determine how many students make up a specific subgroup that must be counted. If 35 students make up a subgroup, there will be many more schools with special education subgroups that must make AYP than if a subgroup consists of 40, 50, or 60 students. Schools with only 39 special education students, for example, would not have a special education subgroup if a subgroup were defined as 40 students.

There are supporters and detractors of *NCLB*, especially as it relates to special education students. Some are concerned that the scores of special education students will lower the scores of an entire school, resulting in sanctions for that school. Others are concerned that requiring these students to take the same tests as other students is unfair, overwhelming, and may lead to a higher dropout rate. Another viewpoint is that spending the time in academics and test preparation will take time away from the vocational and life skills training students with disabilities usually need.

Supporters of *NCLB* feel that holding special education students to the same standards is appropriate, necessary, and will result in these students achieving at a higher level. They assert that raising expectations will force schools to improve the way they teach special education students and will result in graduates that can function well and hold jobs in the future.

One point of conflict is that *NCLB* and IDEA seem to have very different philosophies. IDEA focuses on the individual needs of students with disabilities. These needs may not correlate with the requirements of the state standards or standardized tests. *NCLB* focuses on attaining the standards and having high expectations for all students, including those with disabilities.

Elements of Successful Inclusion

When inclusion works well, children with disabilities become members of their classroom communities, valued for their abilities and for who they are. In a fully inclusive school, the term 'special education' is rarely used.

Proponents of "full inclusion" believe that it should be the regular classroom teacher's responsibility to educate children with disabilities. The regular classroom teacher must learn how to adapt the classroom to accommodate the child with a disability and needs the necessary technical assistance. In an ideal inclusive classroom, the regular teacher and a support specialist work together in an arrangement that best meets an individual student's needs. This can range from occasional technical support to full-time classroom assistance.

In an inclusion model, disabled students sometimes leave the regular classroom to receive support services, but they do not leave just because they are learning at a different rate or with different materials from their classmates.

The major benefits of inclusion for disabled children are higher academic expectations and accomplishments and the development of better socialization skills. There are benefits for non-disabled children, too, who learn to accept human differences. Disabled students often grow academically as a result of collaborative teaching and the use of innovative teaching strategies and regular classroom techniques. Inclusion gives all students opportunities to interact with a variety of people. Non-disabled students can develop a sense of responsibility and increased self-esteem when working with disabled peers.

One of the main advantages for non-disabled students is that they can learn to overcome their stereotypes, prejudices, and misconceptions about students with disabilities. Teachers in an inclusive classroom must not allow disabled students to become the source of jokes or victims of teasing and ridicule. This is one of the major problems for disabled students in a regular classroom setting.

At the end of this chapter is a sample unit entitled "Understanding Disabilities" that increases understanding and helps students overcome misconceptions about disabilities. **The Individual Lesson Plan**™ **(ILP)** format gives Student Choices in the learning activities based on this theme. The sample Questivities™ shows how to develop one Student Choice activity in depth to further students' understanding of disabilities and their disabled classmates.

Successful inclusion takes time. Schools need to establish it gradually. Teachers need time to talk with one another and work out strategies for dealing with disabled children. Collaboration with specialists and receiving adequate training to work with disabled children are two necessary elements for a successful inclusion program. When regular education and special education teachers can work in teams, when there is a full and equal partnership between the teachers, and when they plan lessons together and collaborate to individualize instruction, inclusion is much more likely to work.

Inclusion works best when it is part of several other reforms such as team teaching, peer teaching, cooperative learning, authentic assessment, multi-age classes, middle school structures, access to innovative technology, and thematic interdisciplinary instruction. It thrives where there is good communication, a culture of innovation, and a philosophy of differentiation for all students. When inclusion works best, all teachers collaborate and learn new skills that in turn benefit all students.

Strategies for Beginning a Successful Inclusion Program

Teacher Reflection Page

Before beginning an inclusion program and at the beginning of each school year, discuss and act upon the issues listed below. Take time to share these items with your colleagues.

1. Schedule planning and collaboration time. Special education and regular education teachers need time to share concerns and areas of expertise. This cannot be done in five minutes while walking down the hallway!

2. Consider your own attitude and the attitudes of other teachers regarding meeting the needs of disabled students, and communicate the benefits of inclusion to their parents.

3. Look at students with disabilities as people first. Concentrate on other attributes rather than the disability. For example, instead of saying, *"My deaf student"* refer to the student as *"My student who loves cats"* or *"My student who can never find a pencil."* All students with disabilities have other attributes besides the disability.

4. Be willing to collaborate with and teach with another teacher. You must adjust and compromise on some things, but you will learn many new things from your colleague, too.

5. Don't be afraid to ask for help. Contrary to popular opinion, this is not a sign of weakness. Other professionals routinely consult colleagues, especially about difficult cases. Teachers should do the same.

6. Discuss logistics such as scheduling, paperwork, use of materials, ways of grouping students, etc. Decide the 'nuts and bolts' issues ahead of time. When teaching with another teacher, watch for gaps and overlaps. A gap occurs when each of you assumes the other is responsible for a given task and the task does not get done. An overlap occurs when both of you do the same task that only needed to be done once.

7. Visit other classrooms and other schools to see how they are implementing inclusion. You will gain good ideas and will learn from their mistakes. There is no need to "reinvent the wheel." Learn from others!

8. Make sure the non-disabled students have their needs met, and communicate the benefits of inclusion for them to their parents.

9. Learn differentiation strategies. These often work well with disabled students.

10. Brainstorm strategies for dealing with standards, standardized tests, and other assessments. Modifications are usually needed for disabled students.

© Carolyn Coil

Problems and Concerns About Inclusion

A potential negative aspect of inclusion is that teachers sometimes receive inadequate resources and are not involved in the planning about how to work with disabled students. Some teachers report that suddenly several disabled students are "dumped" into their classes and that they have had no training in how to deal with them. It is easy to see why teachers feel resentful of such a practice!

Ideally, every school that decides to implement inclusion supplies all of the assistance teachers need to make it successful. However, some schools begin inclusion without the needed support, and when the support and resources are not there, terrible problems can develop. For example, IEPs are sometimes withheld from regular teachers even though they are responsible for the modifications in instruction and testing stated on the IEP. If regular teachers are not informed about their students' disabilities and special needs, disastrous consequences often are the result. When the administration or school district provides no training for regular classroom teachers, they rightly feel inadequate and resentful.

Maintaining proper support for children with disabilities and those who teach them requires a great degree of commitment, communication, and skill. Assigning disabled children to regular classrooms because of budget cuts is not the way to make inclusion work successfully. Inclusion is never merely a cost-cutting approach. Nor is it good to have token inclusion that isolates the disabled child in the classroom and provides no peers with a similar special need. Additionally, if a special education teacher has 20 students who are dispersed into 10 different classrooms, it is difficult to see how true collaboration can happen. Clustering groups of disabled students into a few classrooms with a well-trained regular classroom teacher is usually a better strategy.

Peer tutoring can be a successful strategy in an inclusive classroom. A word of caution – don't overuse it. If it becomes the predominant mode of instruction, this is not beneficial or fair to the students doing the tutoring nor to the disabled students being tutored.

The goal of providing equal educational opportunities through inclusion often comes face-to-face with the practical concerns of implementing this philosophy in the classroom. Some issues include:

- Administrative support
- Specialized training
- Paraprofessional assistance
- Being overwhelmed by the demands of teaching a disabled child
- Managing an environment filled with even more diverse needs than are already present in a typical classroom
- Encouraging diversity and equity yet providing instructional excellence
- Participation in inclusion - must all teachers be involved?
- Is this just another idea that will fade with time?
- Dealing with a student whose behavior is dangerous/disruptive to others
- Documenting gains in academic and social skills for disabled students
- Impact of *NCLB* regarding disabled students

Magnet Enriched Classrooms: An Inclusion Model That Works

The Kids Are People School, a private preschool/elementary school in Boston, Massachusetts, has successfully integrated "typical needs" and "special needs" children for over 20 years. Both groups, disabled or not, represent diverse backgrounds and intelligences. The Director of this school does not believe in "forced inclusion." In fact, she thinks this is the worst thing we can do to children. Instead, in a Magnet Enriched Classroom only those teachers who are comfortable with special needs and who have faith in their abilities to work with such students can apply for the job of inclusion classroom teacher. For more information, visit www.greatschools.net.

Like the magnet schools concept, implementing Magnet Enriched Classrooms within each school (such as the ones described above) involves including both disabled and non-disabled students in an enriched educational environment. The low student/teacher ratio and innovative instructional approaches in this type of classroom appeal to many parents and to non-disabled students who differ in ability just as disabled students do.

Teachers use physical space in innovative ways. Specialists, classroom teachers and paraprofessionals co-teach and have training and planning time together. This model envisions a learning environment filled with ideas, energy, and resources. Only teachers who truly want to participate in the inclusion of special needs children are selected for the magnet classroom assignment.

Magnet classrooms must provide a full menu of choices for students. Such classrooms benefit from a student-centered curriculum characterized by adaptability, flexibility, and personalization for each student. They incorporate the ideal of high expectations for all students, with teachers knowing how to "push" and knowing how to praise. In the Magnet Enriched Classroom setting, perseverance is important for both teachers and students.

The "Secret Techniques" Myth

Special education teachers do not possess some secret or magic teaching technique that they use with their students that other teachers know nothing about. Good teachers of special needs students do what good teachers of all students do. They are sensitive to individual problems and needs. They diversify and modify techniques, materials, activities, assignments, and assessment. They differentiate instruction based on student need.

Special education students are more similar to "regular" students than they are different. Most are just as capable of learning. Students with learning disabilities and behavior disorders, for instance, possess ingenuity, creativity, and intelligence as much as any other group of students. Their disabilities, however, have often interfered with their ability or desire to learn. This does not have to be the case. It can change as good regular classroom teachers work with these students and collaborate regularly with the special education teachers.

Modifying and Adapting Educational Materials and Teaching Techniques

One successful strategy for inclusion is to modify and adapt the materials and teaching techniques you are currently using in your classroom. If you are a regular education teacher, ask the special education teacher to help you. Often special education teachers will have materials they have already adapted and can offer suggestions for new techniques. Making minor alterations can sometimes result in a big difference in the possibilities of success for a student with disabilities. Below are some easily implemented suggestions for modifying and adapting materials and teaching techniques.

1. Present work in smaller amounts. Give students with disabilities smaller increments of work at a time. This helps the student who is overwhelmed by a large assignment.

2. Make a special loose-leaf workbook for your disabled student so that all of his or her papers can be kept in one place.

3. Mark pages that need to be done with a paper clip or self-stick note.

4. Secure work to the student's desk with masking tape.

5. Allow the student to underline or circle answers instead of writing them. Encourage the use of highlighters and other writing tools.

6. If the student has trouble copying items from the board, have the assignment written out for him/her ahead of time.

7. Adapt the amount of work required depending on the pace the student is able to set for the task at hand.

8. Keep materials on a shelf or locker except for the ones the student is currently using.

9. Adjust the physical arrangements of your classroom in any way that might help students with disabilities. This includes knowing the best viewing distance for reading print materials, locations that facilitate hearing and lip reading, adaptations for physical impairments, etc.

10. Provide visual tools such as outlines, concept maps, and other visual organizers that students can use to help direct their thinking.

11. Use technological tools to support learning. Examples are listed below.

- **Adaptive computer devices**

- **Tape recorders for storytelling, data collection, and oral journals**

- **Word processors and graphics programs**

- **Computer software and online resources for individual pacing of learning**

- **Voice recognition software**

- **Speech synthesizers**

- **Books on tape or CD-Rom**

- **Calculators**

- **Electronic organizers or PDAs**

- **Assistive Technology devices**

> *For more information on technology, see Chapter 14. Also, contact the Council for Exceptional Children (CEC), 1110 North Glebe Road, Suite 300, Arlington, VA 22201*
> *Voice phone: 703/620-3660*
> *TTY: 866/915-5000*
> *FAX: 703/264-9494*
> *E-mail: service@ced.sped.org*
> *Internet: www.cec.sped.org*

Understanding Disabilities

Write a short story about a day in your life pretending you have a disability or an actual day in your life if you are disabled.

Spend a day in a wheelchair. Demonstrate problems you had.

Demonstrate a technological device that is specifically designed to assist persons with disabilities.

Read a biography about a famous disabled person. Design a book jacket with a picture of the person & summary of his/her life.

Investigate ways technology has allowed persons with disabilities to do many more things. Report your findings to your class.

Learn the braille alphabet. Write a paragraph in braille. Use a braille writer if available at your school.

Make a video of the Special Olympics in your area. Interview Special Olympics athletes.

Make a chart about one type of disability. Include things that persons with this disability CAN do.

On audio tape interview a classmate or someone else in your school with a disability. Find out their challenges and successes.

Learn to sing a song in sign language. Perform the song for your class.

Find out about learning disabilities. Explain this disability to your class through a skit or role play.

Look for places in your school that are not accessible to physically disabled people. Draw a diagram or plan showing how they could become accessible.

© Carolyn Coil

INDIVIDUAL LESSON PLAN - Understanding Disabilities

ACTIVITIES - STUDENT CHOICES

Visual

1. Make a chart about one type of disability. Include things that persons with this disability CAN do.

2. Look for places in your school that are not accessible to physically disabled people. Draw a diagram or plan showing how they could become accessible.

3. Read a biography about a famous disabled person. Design a book jacket with a picture of the person & summary of his/her life.

Verbal

7. On audio tape interview a classmate or someone else in your school with a disability. Find out their challenges and successes.

8. Write a short story about a day in your life pretending you have a disability or an actual day in your life if you are disabled.

9. Find out about learning disabilities. Explain this disability to your class through a skit or role play.

Kinesthetic

4. Learn to sing a song in sign language. Perform the song for your class.

5. Spend a day in a wheelchair. Demonstrate problems you had.

6. Learn the braille alphabet. Write a paragraph in braille. Use a braille writer if available at your school.

Technological

10. Investigate ways technology has allowed persons with disabilities to do many more things. Report your findings to your class.

11. Demonstrate a technological device that is specifically designed to assist persons with disabilities.

12. Make a video of the Special Olympics in your area. Interview Special Olympics athletes.

Required Activities Teacher's Choice

1. Listen to a Special Education teacher talk about types of disabilities and the inclusion model in your classroom. Write your questions about disabilities on index cards.

2. Collect 3 news stories about people with disabilities. Write a summary of each.

3. View the "Kids on the Block" puppet show. Participate in follow-up activities.

Product/Performance Required

1. Questions on index cards

2. Summary of news stories

3. Follow-up activities

Assessment Required Activities

1. Observation from discussion about questions

2. Comprehension of stories

3. Active participation

Optional Student-Parent Cooperative Activity

Find out about a relative with a disability. What are his/her problems? successes? Make a scrapbook about this person.

Student Choices in Ways to Learn

Visual _____

Verbal _____

Kinesthetic _____

Technological _____

Product/Performance Student Choice

Standards

Due Date Student Choice

Learning Modality

- Technological

Learning Style

- Concrete Random

Taxonomy Level

- Application

Multiple Intelligence

- Bodily/Kinesthetic
- Interpersonal
- Visual/Spatial
- Verbal/Linguistic

Assessment Mini-Rubric

- Equipment working
- Ability to use
- Clear explanation of function

Project Question

- In what ways can technology be used to make life better for people with disabilities?

Understanding Disabilities Questivities™

Project Activity

Demonstrate a technological device that is specifically designed to assist persons with disabilities. Explain how it works and how it helps a disabled person.

Questivities™ Thinking Questions

1. List all the types of technological devices that may help people with disabilities.
2. Compare/contrast a battery-run wheelchair with a wheelchair that has no battery.
3. How is a robot like a guide dog?
4. What new technological devices could be invented to help persons with disabilities?
5. What would happen if you invented a new device for disabled people?
6. Why do some people with disabilities use a head pointer?
7. How could a technological device help some paraplegics walk again?

Active Question

Make a list of questions a speech synthesizer might ask a tape recorder.

Directions: Answer the Questivities™ Thinking Questions and the Active Question before doing the Project Activity.

Strategies for Successful Inclusion

Teacher Reflection Page

Listed below are a number of strategies and techniques to use in building a school and classroom climate where inclusion models can be successfully implemented. Consider each item listed. To what extent does this already exist in your school or classroom? If you are already using it, what could you do differently to increase its effectiveness? If you are not currently using the strategy, how could you begin to implement it?

❑ 1. Hands-on teaching

❑ 2. Combination of child-directed and teacher-directed activities

❑ 3. Teacher as the facilitator of learning

❑ 4. Multi-age classes

❑ 5. Individualized instruction

❑ 6. Cooperative learning

❑ 7. Peer tutoring or buddy system

❑ 8. Modifying and adapting educational materials

❑ 9. Innovative use of classroom space

❑ 10. Use of technological tools

❑ 11. Low child-to-teacher ratio

❑ 12. Alternative assessment

❑ 13. Collaboration between teachers

❑ 14. Differentiation strategies focusing on strengths in learning modalities, multiple intelligences, and learning styles

❑ 15. Using the "Understanding Disabilities" thematic unit found on the next three pages

Reflections

* Federal laws, including *NCLB*, have a major impact on the education of children with disabilities.

* Inclusion is an educational philosophy based on the belief that all students, including students with disabilities, are to participate fully in their school community.

* The practice of inclusion has become more common in schools throughout the United States.

* Inclusion works best when there is adequate teacher training, time for true collaboration between teachers, and an abundance of human and material resources.

* Maintaining a high level of support for both teachers and students is essential if inclusion is to be successful.

Notes _____

Chapter 11

Educating Gifted Students

Questions to Consider

1. What does gifted mean? Which students are gifted?

2. What types of learning activities and programs do gifted students need?

3. What strategies can I use to differentiate for gifted students in the regular classroom?

4. Which type of grouping is best for gifted students?

5. What can school districts do to develop a good gifted program?

Jac is in first grade and has been reading for years. At 18 months he could read labels and signs, and in the summer between kindergarten and first grade he read five volumes of C.S. Lewis' "Chronicles of Narnia" series. Jac's first grade teacher is at a loss about how to teach him.

Shaundra is a 7th grader who is a high achiever. She is a straight A student who works rapidly and invariably completes her assignments before the rest of the class. The teacher often asks her to help by tutoring slower students.

Maria is quite artistic. She is an independent learner who "sneaks" books to read during class but doesn't always finish her assigned work. She doodles when she should be taking notes and draws clever, humorous cartoons that are very popular with her classmates.

Rebellious Greg refuses to do his assigned work in school. He is considered a behavior problem by his teachers and makes poor grades on his report card. Yet he tests in the gifted range on standardized IQ tests. The guidance counselor at his school calls him a "classic underachiever."

Who are the Gifted?

All four of the students described above are gifted, yet they are very different and individualistic in their abilities and educational needs. Gifted students range from the highly gifted to the cooperative "teacher's pet," and from the artist to the rebellious underachiever. No wonder it is difficult to say exactly who gifted students are!

For over 40 years, American educators have struggled to define what being gifted means. In 1972, the U.S. Office of Education issued the Marland Report. This report concluded there are at least six categories of gifted and talented children "who by virtue of outstanding abilities are capable of high performance." From this came the Federal law (Public Law 91-230) that defines gifted and talented children in five of the original six categories:

- General intellectual ability
- Specific academic aptitude
- Creative or productive thinking
- Leadership ability
- Visual/performing arts

This law also recommends differentiation as it states:

"These are children who require differentiated educational programs and/or services beyond those normally provided by the regular school programs to realize their contribution to self and society."

Gifted students are those who *perform* or *show promise of performing* at high levels in any of the five categories listed above. They need special programs and services to ensure the *growth* rather than the *loss* of their outstanding abilities. Giftedness can be found in children from all cultural, ethnic, and socioeconomic groups.

Many of the theories discussed earlier in this book can help broaden our vision of gifts and talents. However, we must be careful not to fall into the trap of thinking "all kids are gifted." All children possess learning strengths and weaknesses, but this does not mean that all are far above the norm. Consider the theories discussed in previous chapters as you consider giftedness, but remember to look at the level, intensity, or uniqueness that sets a gifted child apart from his or her peers.

States, and sometimes individual school districts, construct their own definition of giftedness and decide whether to mandate programs for gifted and talented students. Therefore, you will find great variety in the definition of gifted, identification methods, programs, and services offered for gifted students in school districts throughout the United States. You will also discover many different opinions about which students are actually gifted.

For many years, districts identified a disproportionate number of white middle class and upper middle class students as gifted while they did not identify many minority students as gifted. Some states have changed their definition and their eligibility criteria so that gifted programs are more inclusive. In 1996, the state of Georgia, for example, began including four categories of eligibility for gifted. These are Mental Ability, Achievement, Creativity, and Motivation. A student must meet criteria in three of the four categories to be eligible for gifted programs and services. Before 1996, Georgia only included the category of Mental Ability in its criteria. This multiple criteria has increased the number of minority students identified as gifted.

Needs of Gifted Students

A "one size fits all" curriculum actually fits no one. This is especially true for gifted and talented students. In order for them to reach their potential so that they can be the leaders in academia, business, and the arts in the 21st century, they should work and study hard to master challenging knowledge and skills. Unfortunately, the message gifted students often get is to drift through school and aim for mediocrity, proficiency, or minimum competency, not excellence.

According to "National Excellence: A Case for Developing America's Talent," a report issued in 1993 by the U.S. Department of Education, most gifted and talented students spend their school days without much attention given to their specific learning needs. Consider these findings cited in the report:

- **Gifted and talented elementary school students have mastered from 35 to 50 percent of the curriculum offered in five basic subjects before they begin the school year.**

- Most regular classroom teachers make few, if any, provisions for gifted and talented students.

- Most of the highest achieving students in the nation included in Who's Who Among American High School Students reported that they studied less than an hour a day.

It is easy to see why so many gifted students say they are bored in school!

No Child Left Behind (NCLB) and Gifted Students

The No Child Left Behind (NCLB) law focuses both attention and resources on closing the achievement gap. Its goal is for all students to reach proficiency at their grade levels in language arts, reading, and math. The law provides incentives for schools to work hard so that all student subgroups make adequate yearly progress (AYP) toward the goal of proficiency and has consequences if they do not.

However, one subgroup - gifted children - is not considered in NCLB. There are no incentives for advancing students who are already proficient or who are well above grade level on the first day of school. In fact, there are no consequences if such students stand still and make no progress at all! Because NCLB does not address continuous growth and progress for all students, many gifted students seem to be the ones "left behind."

In education, resources are always limited. In some states and districts, funding has been taken away from gifted education in order to concentrate resources on those subgroups that are not as yet proficient and seem to be most in need of help.

Making AYP is almost always measured by standardized test results. Such tests usually focus on basic skills and lower levels of thinking. Because of this, classroom activities addressing higher-level thinking, questioning skills, creativity, initiative, perseverance, research skills, and complex problem solving are sometimes eliminated, especially in low-performing schools. While such activities benefit all students, gifted students in particular need them in order to progress in their learning. Activities such as these with results measured by rich performance assessments are needed in order to see the continuous progress of our most able students. If their learning is measured only by grade level standardized tests, it is impossible to say that "No Gifted Child is Left Behind."

Program and Service Options for Gifted Students

A wide variety of curricula, programs, and services have been developed for gifted students. In general, gifted students can be served in the regular classroom, in special classes, or in a special school. Specific options available to gifted students usually are determined by the offerings of the local school or school district.

The National Association for Gifted Children (NAGC) has developed a set of Gifted Program Standards for Pre-K – Grade 12. These standards recommend a "coordinated and comprehensive structure of informal and formal services provided on a continuing basis." They also recommend a continuum of services rather than a "one-size-fits-all" gifted program. For more information about these standards visit www.nagc.org

Generally, the majority of gifted students are in the regular classroom for most of their time in school. At the elementary level, this may be supplemented by some type of a pull-out or resource class taught by a teacher who is a specialist in gifted education. At the secondary level, gifted students may attend subject-based classes especially for the gifted (such as Gifted Science) or may enroll in Honors, Advanced Placement, Pre-AP, or International Baccalaureate courses. Some gifted high school students take Dual Enrollment college classes where they receive both high school and college credit.

Specialists in gifted education encourage programs and services that provide enrichment, extensions to the general education curriculum, and/or acceleration.

Enrichment consists of experiences and activities that introduce the learner to a variety of topics, processes, and strategies that lead to critical and creative thinking, problem solving, and an interest in new areas of study.

Extensions are explorations of a given topic of study in greater depth and complexity than would be done by general education students. This is the approach most often used in differentiating curriculum for gifted students in a regular classroom setting.

Acceleration indicates progress through the curriculum or educational program at a faster rate or at a younger age than is usually done. **Grade-based acceleration** shortens the number of years a student spends in K-12 education while **subject-based acceleration** allows a student to study advanced content at an earlier age or grade than usual.

A Sampling of Specific Program Models

There are many programs and curricular options that are appropriate for gifted students. The following is a sampling of better-known options.

Advanced Placement (AP) – Begun in 1955, the AP program is one of the fastest growing options for high school students. It provides students with the opportunity to take intense and rigorous academic courses and is generally thought to be good preparation for college work. Run by the College Board, it offers college-level courses to high school students. Students can take AP exams at the end of the year, and if they score high enough (usually a score of 4 or 5 on a 5-point scale) these classes can count for college credit.

Autonomous Learner Model (ALM) – Originally developed in 1978 by Dr. George Betts and Jolene Kercher as a high school model, it has since been modified to extend its use to grades K-12. The goal of the model is to facilitate the growth of students as independent, self-directed learners with the development of skills in the cognitive, emotional, and social domains. The five dimensions of this model are:

1. Orientation
2. Individual Development
3. Enrichment
4. Seminars
5. In-depth Study

International Baccalaureate (IB) – This program was created by a group of parents and teachers at an International School in Geneva, Switzerland, in the 1960s and 1970s. The IB curriculum emphasizes extensive writing and in-depth learning. It also requires public service and completing a philosophy course called The Theory of Knowledge. A special IB diploma, which is recognized all over the world, is issued when students complete the rigorous course work and pass challenging examinations in six subjects. The IB program is now available at the elementary school level (Primary Years Program or PYP) and at the middle school level (Middle Years Program or MYP).

Parallel Curriculum Model (PCM) – Developed by a group of experts in gifted education as a service publication for the National Association for Gifted Children, this curriculum model offers four parallel approaches to curriculum development. The four parallels are:

1. The Core or Basic Curriculum

2. The Curriculum of Connections

3. The Curriculum of Practice

4. The Curriculum of Identity

In each of the four parallels, educators challenge gifted students by offering a variety of pathways toward ascending intellectual demand such as more advanced reading and research, interactions among multiple disciplines, and collaboration with a professional in a given field of study.

Schoolwide Enrichment Model (SEM) – Developed by Dr. Joseph Renzulli as an extension of his earlier Enrichment Triad Model, this model is an approach for total school improvement. Its goal is to provide challenging and high-end learning across the entire school population. The SEM targets the development of strengths in all children and recommends flexibility in differentiating both the standard curriculum and enrichment learning.

A Potpourri of Gifted Program Options

There are many approaches to teaching the gifted and numerous options to use in teaching these students. These may stand alone or may be used in combination with one another.

Regular classroom with cluster grouping – Four to eight gifted students are clustered together in a regular classroom with a teacher who has training in gifted education.

Regular classroom with enrichment activities – Gifted students are offered enrichment activities in the regular classroom setting.

Regular classroom with curriculum compacting – Students are allowed to test out of work they have already mastered, and, instead of regular classroom work, they work on an alternate, more challenging activity.

Regular classroom with telescoping – Students complete the curriculum at a faster pace, such as completing two years of math in one year.

Regular classroom with independent study or learning contracts – Students are in the regular classroom but work independently on projects or individual areas of study.

Regular classroom with consultative services – Gifted students are in the regular classroom full time, but a gifted specialist consults with and gives ideas, suggestions, and/or resources to the regular classroom teacher.

Regular classroom with differentiation – The regular classroom teacher differentiates the curriculum thereby offering appropriate learning options to gifted students.

Multi-age and/or Multi-grade with flexible grouping – Students from two or more grade levels are in the same classroom. The teacher flexibly groups students depending on learning needs.

Full-time gifted class (elementary) – Gifted students at a given grade level are together in a class with a teacher who is trained/certified to teach gifted students. This is a self-contained class for gifted students.

Acceleration to another grade level (part-time) – A gifted student or students are put in a higher grade level for a specific subject. For example, a second-grader goes to 4th grade for math.

Acceleration to another grade level (full-time) – A gifted student or students who skip a grade at the beginning of the school year or who are placed in a higher grade level during the school year.

Gifted resource (pull-out) for enrichment/extension – Gifted students leave the regular classroom and attend a resource class taught by a gifted specialist. This can be every day for a certain amount of time or on different days during the week. The curriculum can be acceleration, an extension of the regular grade-level curriculum, enrichment activities, or a combination of these..

Gifted resource in one or more subjects – Gifted students attend the resource class for a specific subject such as reading, science, social studies, or math. The gifted teacher is responsible for teaching the standards in that particular subject and for giving the report card grade.

Special class (secondary) – Gifted students attend this regularly-scheduled class for the entire class period. The gifted teacher gives the grade for this subject. Gifted Science or Gifted English are examples.

Advanced Placement – High-level courses taught in high school that may count for college credit based on the score on the AP exam.

Honors classes – Higher-level classes taught at middle and high school that are more challenging than regular classes at the same grade level.

Dual Enrollment – College courses that can be taken for both high school and college credit. They are usually taught at a community college but may be at a four-year college or even taught in the high school itself.

Seminars – In-depth discussions on a particular subject that are usually led by an expert in the field. Students are expected to do background reading and research before attending the seminar.

Independent study class – The student completes an in-depth study of a particular topic under the direction and guidance of a teacher.

Shadowing a professional – The student goes to the workplace of a professional and observes this person for a number of days or weeks. Shadowing usually involves discussions with the professional but not hands-on involvement in the work activities.

Mentorship – An individual student is assigned a mentor who will work with the student, answer questions, and guide him through a research project or independent study. Mentors are often professionals from the community.

Executive Internship – The student works with a professional in the community and is given specific job responsibilities in a field of interest.

Group counseling – Usually targeted to affective and social-emotional needs of gifted students, this allows a group of students to discuss issues on an in-depth level.

Magnet school for gifted – A school or school-within-a-school for gifted students. Gifted students from a wide geographical area may attend this school. Students are generally chosen to attend based on test scores, portfolios, by lottery, or by some other application process.

Distance learning/ Online courses – Courses that are offered online, including virtual high schools and online college courses. Distance learning courses where gifted students can join others and take classes not offered at their home school opens up a wider range of choices for many gifted students.

Home schooling – This approach allows for an individualized education to meet the unique needs of a gifted child. The child's education is planned and organized by the parent(s) and usually the parent(s) is the child's main teacher. Many home schooling parents also draw on the resources and expertise of others in the community to help in their child's education.

Academic competitions – Gifted children need to be challenged academically, especially in those areas of intense interest or ability. Academic competitions of all types can be highly motivating and often put gifted children in touch with other like-minded kids.

Options outside of school – Schools should not provide the only educational options for gifted students. Many activities outside of school such as community theater, museum programs, scouts, church youth groups, etc. provide wonderful opportunities for gifted kids.

Summer programs for gifted – There are a vast number of summer programs for gifted and high-ability students. From the Talent Identification Program (TIP) where middle school students are selected based on high SAT scores to programs offered by local colleges and universities, summer programs abound. These may be some of the best learning options gifted children ever have.

Extra-curricular activities – Schools, especially middle and high schools, offer numerous extra-curricular activities. For gifted students, it is more important to pick the activities that hold the most interest than try to go to every program that is offered! Gifted kids can become stressed-out kids with too many activities. They can enjoy enrichment and become well-rounded by having a reasonable number of such activities.

Strategies for Differentiating Curriculum for Gifted Students in the Regular Classroom

Most gifted students spend the majority of their time in school in the regular classroom setting. Since they are not gifted just when they go to the resource class (if such a class exists in their school), it is important that all educators have the tools to meet their needs through differentiating the learning activities in the regular classroom.

Look at the chart on the next page. It summarizes some of the needs and concerns of gifted students along with suggested strategies and techniques that regular classroom teachers can use as tools to differentiate their curriculum and learning activities to meet these needs. Refer also to several other chapters in this book that discuss many of these tools.

DIFFERENTIATION FOR GIFTED STUDENTS

Needs and Concerns		Strategies and Techniques

1. Student already knows the skill or concept that is being taught. →
- ❑ Flexible Grouping
- ❑ Curriculum Compacting
- ❑ Learning Contract
- ❑ Collaboration with other teachers

2. Student will learn the information, skills and/or concepts faster than most others in the class. →
- ❑ Independent study
- ❑ Become a resident expert on some facet of the topic
- ❑ Thematic Units

3. Student could become interested in the topic, but the teaching style does not match his learning style. →
- ❑ Individual Lesson Plans™ (ILP) based on Learning Styles, Learning Modalities and / or Multiple Intelligences

4. Student does not feel she is being academically or intellectually challenged. →
- ❑ Questivities™
- ❑ ILPs™ at the higher levels of Bloom's Taxonomy
- ❑ Enrichment activities that involve real life problem solving
- ❑ Acceleration strategies
- ❑ Tiered Lesson/Units

5. Student has given up on school, is unmotivated, wants to be entertained rather than work. →
- ❑ Pursuit of special interest area
- ❑ Personal interest and attention from one "special teacher"
- ❑ Personal goal setting
- ❑ Development of self-confidence

CURRICULUM COMPACTING

Dr. Joseph Renzulli designed the process of Curriculum Compacting as a way of documenting mastery of the skills and content in the regular classroom while allowing the student more time to complete acceleration and enrichment activities.

On the next page is a sample Compactor Form. Each student who compacts a portion of the curriculum needs a form. Some suggested steps and guidelines for Curriculum Compacting are:

- Begin with part of the regular curriculum that is easy to pretest. Decide what percentage of correct answers students will need in order to 'test out' of the regular classroom work. Any student, not just those identified as gifted, should have the opportunity to take the pretest.

- Refer to your list of state standards. Some of your students may already have mastered them! From them you may be able to identify a number of items to go into the left-hand column of the compactor.

- The *Skill, Knowledge, Benchmark*, or *Standard* column of the Compactor indicates the particular skill, concept or knowledge the student has mastered.

- Use the second column of the Compactor to record the pretest score or any other evidence you have used to show mastery.

- The Alternate Activities are those activities the student will work on while the rest of the class is completing grade-level work. These can be from the same subject area or can involve the student's particular area of interest. Look at activities from an Individual Lesson Plan™ (ILP) or from the Questivities™ found in this book for suggestions and ideas.

- Assess the Alternate Activities completed by the student by using some type of authentic assessment criteria (see Chapter 6). However, the grade given for the activity should be the grade on the pretest plus additional points for Alternate Activities. A student should never be penalized grade-wise for working on more difficult work.

- Each student should keep a folder, box, portfolio, or other organizer containing the Compactor Form and all of the work completed in the Alternate Activities. Learning to be responsible for these items is an important element of this strategy.

- Alternate Activities should be Student Choice activities. Do not tell the student he or she must use the time to remediate an area of weakness. Compactor time is valuable time for gifted students to work at their own level and pace on something of interest to them!

- Set rules and guidelines for behavior and plan some of your time to work with Compactor students. Compactor time is not free time or play time!

- Check frequently on Compactor activities to offer suggestions and monitor progress.

- Working independently on a Compactor assignment is an excellent way for gifted students to develop organization and time management skills. However, they may need help in this area. Do not assume they already know these skills!

CURRICULUM COMPACTOR FORM

Student's Name _____

Skill, Knowledge, Benchmark or Standard	Documentation of Mastery	Student Choice Alternate Activities

The most important rule for a student working in a Compactor is . . .
The one choice you never have is the choice to do nothing!

USING THE LEARNING CONTRACT

Another tool that works well with many gifted students is the Learning Contract. Learning Contracts are formalized agreements between the student and the teacher about the work the student will be doing during a unit of study. Learning Contracts for gifted students generally allow for acceleration, extensions/enrichment or both.

Acceleration in a Learning Contract allows the student to study the material at a faster pace and/or at a higher grade level than would normally be the case. Collaborating with another teacher at a higher grade level is one way to acquire information and resources to use in acceleration. Accelerated learning activities can be done within the regular classroom, by going to another classroom, with a mentor or other adult volunteer, or by attending another school for a portion of the day.

Enrichment and extension activities include studying areas of the topic or other interest areas that are not included in the regular curriculum. Often this means delving into a subject more deeply. Many Student Choice activities in the **Individual Lesson Plans**™ **(ILP)** are appropriate as enrichment and extension activities for gifted students.

There are many types of Learning Contracts. Usually they list the work or study a student agrees to do. Most also include rules, working conditions, expectations for behavior, time management, and due dates. Contracts of all kinds generally include signatures. The same is true for Learning Contracts. Having both the teacher and the student sign the Learning Contract creates a formal agreement for student work.

You will find one type of Learning Contract on the next two pages. Page 173 is an example of a contract used by a middle school student. A blank form is on the following page. This Learning Contract contains the following elements:

- **Required activities the student will do with the rest of the class**

- **Options for acceleration**

- **Options for enrichment/extensions**

- **Rules/terms of the contract**

- **Checkpoint dates**

- **Signatures**

Checkpoint Dates are the dates on which the teacher will look at the progress the student is making. Use this for formative assessments and to help the student stay on task. This will lessen the chances of procrastination and last minute panic!

LEARNING CONTRACT for _____ (Name of Student)

Subject/Thematic Unit/Topic _____Amphibians_____

Required activities to be done by the entire class:

Date	Activity
_____	Do a written report on amphibians
_____	Read background information on topic from textbook
_____	Participate in "Frog Day" interdisciplinary activities

Acceleration Options

Check your
choice(s)

_____	Define high school amphibian vocabulary words
_____	Do computerized frog dissection
_____	

Enrichment/Extension Options

Check your
choice(s)

_____	Make and label drawings of six rare frogs
_____	Research and do a presentation about why some frogs are becoming extinct
_____	

Rules/Terms of Contract

The one choice you never have is to do nothing

You can move around the room to get materials

Store work on top of the bookshelf

Work in class and at home

Teacher Signature _____

Student Signature _____

Contract Checkpoint Dates

_____
1st day assigned

_____
3rd day

_____
Day before due

LEARNING CONTRACT for _____ ✏

Subject/Thematic Unit/Topic _____

Required activities to be done by the entire class:

Date   Activity

_____   _____

_____   _____

_____   _____

Acceleration Options

Check your
choice(s)

_____   _____

_____   _____

_____   _____

Enrichment/ Extension Options

Check your
choice(s)

_____   _____

_____   _____

_____   _____

Rules/Terms of Contract	**Contract Checkpoint Dates**
_____	_____
_____	_____
_____	_____
_____	_____

Teacher Signature_____

Student Signature _____

Flexible Grouping:
An Effective Teaching Tool with Gifted Students

There has been much discussion and conflicting opinions in recent years about the best way to group gifted students in school. I believe that each of the various forms of grouping can be effective. Why throw away any of these forms? Instead, think of instructional groups as flexible, not permanent, and use and change them as circumstances dictate. Your question should be, *"What are the learning outcomes for this activity and what is the best way to group students for these outcomes to occur?"*

Homogeneous/Ability/Cluster Grouping

This type of grouping clusters students of similar ability or interest. Use it for remediation, acceleration, and enrichment. One way to structure such groups is by multi-grade levels. Dr. Karen Rogers, an expert in ability grouping, supports its benefit for gifted students. Her research shows that almost any way of grouping gifted students together, full or part time, will produce substantial academic gains when compared to equally gifted children who are never grouped by ability. Cluster grouping is a type of homogeneous grouping in which four to eight gifted students are placed in the same classroom with a teacher who has special training in teaching gifted students.

Heterogeneous/Mixed Ability Grouping

This type of grouping combines students of differing abilities or interests. It facilitates the learning of common objectives or standards and works best when reading levels or math proficiencies are not involved. It is good for group projects promoting creativity and can be used with cooperative learning, small group discussion, role playing, and affective curriculum. It is generally a good option when the learning outcome is for students to see many different points of view. Gifted students often benefit when grouped heterogeneously by age and homogeneously by ability and/or interest area.

Heterogeneous grouping provides gifted students with opportunities for peer tutoring, learning to work in teams, leadership development, and improves socialization and understanding between students. A word of caution. In heterogeneous groups, gifted students often become peer tutors for other students. Use peer tutoring sparingly with gifted students. They should not spend the majority of their time in school tutoring others. With heterogeneous grouping, learning objectives and outcomes may be different for gifted students. For example, developing leadership skills may be the outcome in a mixed ability group. (See the next page for an assessment instrument for leadership skills.) Gifted students should never do all of the work in their heterogeneous group and should not be penalized if the quality of work the rest of the group does is not up to standards.

Individualized Instruction/Independent Study

This type of grouping facilitates the management of many achievement levels. It involves self-paced learning at each student's performance level, and can be used for remediation, enrichment, or acceleration. It is good to use in exploring each student's interest areas and can be used in learning skills (such as math skills) at a student's own pace. Computer assisted instruction and distance learning are types of individualized instruction done via technology. Individualized instruction teaches independent learning and helps develop individual responsibility, organizational skills, and time management skills. It must be monitored and appropriately evaluated. (See the Learning Contract on the previous pages as an example of how to implement this strategy.) Independent study is a form of individualized instruction in which a student studies a particular topic in depth.

Whole Class Instruction

This "old fashioned" method is both efficient and effective when presenting new content that all need to know. It works well with many types of audiovisual presentations, for initial instruction, and some enrichment activities. It is appropriate to include all students when you are doing a highly motivational activity. Use whole class instruction for guest speakers, classroom celebrations, and when you are lecturing on your favorite topic.

Leadership and the Gifted

When gifted students are in heterogeneous groups, sometimes the learning outcomes for them will be different than the rest of the group. One approach is to use time in heterogeneous groups to develop their leadership skills. The checklist below is one instrument you can use when you are working to develop your students' leadership skills.

Group Leadership Checklist

As the leader of your group, you will be assessed on the following:

_____ 1. You delegated jobs so that everyone participated in doing the group project or assignment.

_____ 2. You helped the group use time wisely and have good time management skills.

_____ 3. You helped the group plan the project, breaking the big task into smaller parts.

_____ 4. You led the group in making decisions in an orderly way.

_____ 5. You listened to suggestions from everyone.

_____ 6. You made sure the group stayed on task during discussions.

_____ 7. You led the group in brainstorming ideas, making sure all ideas and points of view were considered.

_____ 8. You did not allow put-downs for different thinking.

_____ 9. You helped the group establish rules for dealing with conflicts or differences of opinion.

_____ 10. You treated everyone fairly.

Gifted Students as Resident Experts

The Resident Expert strategy is a type of Independent Study. Gifted students often have certain areas of interest that they would like to explore in greater depth. To facilitate this study, encourage gifted students to become Resident Experts in the topics of their choice. Use the form below to help structure their work.

Resident Expert Planning Form

Name: _____

Topic: _____

Things I already know about this topic: (Use other side of paper if needed)

What I want to learn about this topic:

Resources I could use:

My learning plan with checkpoint dates:

Checkpoint date	Activity
_____ 1.	_____
	_____
_____ 2.	_____
	_____
_____ 3.	_____
	_____
_____ 4.	_____
	_____

Tiered Lessons and Units

Tiered assignments allow students of varying abilities or readiness to work on the same basic content and standards but at different levels. Therefore, tiered lessons are a good option for gifted students in mixed-ability classes. Gifted students who view schoolwork as too easy can become unmotivated and often do not develop the work habits, organizational skills, and study skills they need. Tiered assignments address these concerns and challenge gifted students because teachers can target activities at the appropriate level while also providing suitable activities for other students in the class. On the next several pages you will find Guidelines for Planning, an Initial Planning Form, a sample tiered lesson plan about paragraph writing, and a blank tiered lesson planning form.

Guidelines for Planning Tiered Lessons or Units

1. Establish which standards, objectives, knowledge, or skills all students need to know. Use your state's standards documents to guide you.

2. Make a list of all the activities you have done with students in the past to reach these standards or objectives.

3. Add more activities to your list as you brainstorm with other teachers or get ideas from the textbook or other resources.

4. Decide which of these are appropriate learning activities for all students. These will become your whole class activities.

5. Some of the activities on your list will most likely be easier than others. Put an indication of the level or tier you think each activity might be. You may have two or three levels, but occasionally will have four.

6. Think about ways to expand or extend the easier activities so they will be challenging for gifted and high-ability students and ways to simplify the more difficult activities so that your struggling students can complete them successfully.

7. Look carefully at your list of activities. Many times you will have more activities than your students could possibly do given the amount of time you have for the unit. Decide which activities are essential and which could be eliminated if necessary. Save a few of the activities you eliminate to use with students who finish their work early.

8. Check again to make sure all activities will lead to students learning the standards and objectives.

9. Make sure that activities at all levels are engaging and interesting. Nothing discourages achievement faster than students thinking that the other group is the one with the fun, interesting, or enjoyable activity while the learning activity they have been assigned is not.

10. Write your unit or lesson plan using the Tiered Lesson Plan format.

11. Plan daily lessons based on your Tiered Lesson or Unit plan.

12. Gather supplies and resources needed to carry out the activities.

Initial Planning Form for a Tiered Unit

Theme or Topic:_____

Standards/Benchmarks: _____

_____

_____

_____

Possible Student Activities   Level Of Difficulty

1. _____   _____

   _____   _____

2. _____   _____

   _____   _____

3. _____   _____

   _____   _____

4. _____   _____

   _____   _____

5. _____   _____

   _____   _____

6. _____   _____

   _____   _____

7. _____   _____

   _____   _____

8. _____   _____

   _____   _____

9. _____   _____

   _____   _____

Tiered Lesson Plan: Paragraph Writing

Objectives or Standards

1. Students will write complete sentences beginning with capital letters and ending with correct punctuation.
2. Students will use the correct paragraph format with topic sentence, detail sentences and concluding sentence.

Whole Class Activities

1. Teacher will review what makes a good sentence, emphasizing capital letters, sentence structure and punctuation.

2. Teacher will demonstrate how a paragraph is constructed with topic sentence, detail sentences and a concluding sentence.

3. Class will brainstorm ideas for paragraph topics.

4. Class will pick one topic and together will write a paragraph on this topic using the board, chart paper or overhead.

Assessment

❑ All listening and asking questions as appropriate.

❑ All observing teacher's demonstration.

❑ All students participating.

Level 1 Activities

1. Students will choose a topic from the topics brainstormed by the class. Teacher will help them write a topic sentence. Each student will then write three detail sentences and a concluding sentence for the paragraph.

2. Students will edit their paragraphs with the help of the teacher.

3. Each student will draw a picture to illustrate his or her paragraph.

Assessment

☞ ❑ Has three detail sentences.
❑ All students participating.
❑ Has a concluding sentence.
❑ Sentences support the topic sentence.

☞ ❑ Sentences are complete.
❑ Correct spelling, punctuation and grammar.

☞ ❑ Picture is creative.
❑ Neatly done.
❑ Goes along with the paragraph.

from Standards-Based Activities and Assessments for the Differentiated Classroom by Carolyn Coil. Pieces of Learning.

Level 2 Activities

1. Each student will choose a topic from the topics brainstormed by the class. Each will write a paragraph with a topic sentence, four detail sentences and a concluding sentence.

2. Students will work with a partner to edit and revise their paragraphs.

3. Each student will draw a picture to illustrate his or her paragraph.

Assessment

☞ ❏Has a topic sentence.
❏Four detail sentences.
❏Concluding sentence that supports the topic sentence.

☞ ❏Sentences are complete.
❏Correct spelling, punctuation and grammar.

☞ ❏Picture is creative.
❏Neatly done.
❏Goes along with the paragraph.

Level 3 Activities

1. Each student will choose a topic from the topics brainstormed by the class. Each will write two or three paragraphs on the topic, each with a topic sentence, detail sentences and a concluding sentence.

2. Students will edit and revise their own paragraphs.

3. Each student will draw a picture to illustrate his or her paragraphs.

Assessment

☞ ❏Each paragraph has a topic sentence.
❏Detail sentences and a concluding sentence supports the topic sentence.
❏All paragraphs are about the topic.

☞ ❏Sentences are complete.
❏Correct spelling, punctuation and grammar.

☞ ❏Picture is creative.
❏Neatly done.
❏Goes along with the topic chosen.

Whole Class Culminating Activities

1. Students will work in heterogeneous groups reading their paragraphs and sharing their illustrations.

2. Students will make a list of "Hints for Good Editing" and put it on a poster. Posters from all groups will be hung around the room for future reference.

Assessment

☞ ❏Group participation.
❏Ability to read own writing.
❏Clear presentation.
❏Ability to listen to others.

☞ ❏Follows Poster criteria card.
❏Has at least five suggestions for good editing.

from *Standards-Based Activities and Assessments for the Differentiated Classroom* by Carolyn Coil. *Pieces of Learning.*

Tiered Lesson Plan: Unit Planning Form

Objectives or Standards

1.
2.
3.
4.

Whole Class Activities

Assessment

Level 1 Activities

Assessment

from Standards-Based Activities and Assessments for the Differentiated Classroom by Carolyn Coil. Pieces of Learning.

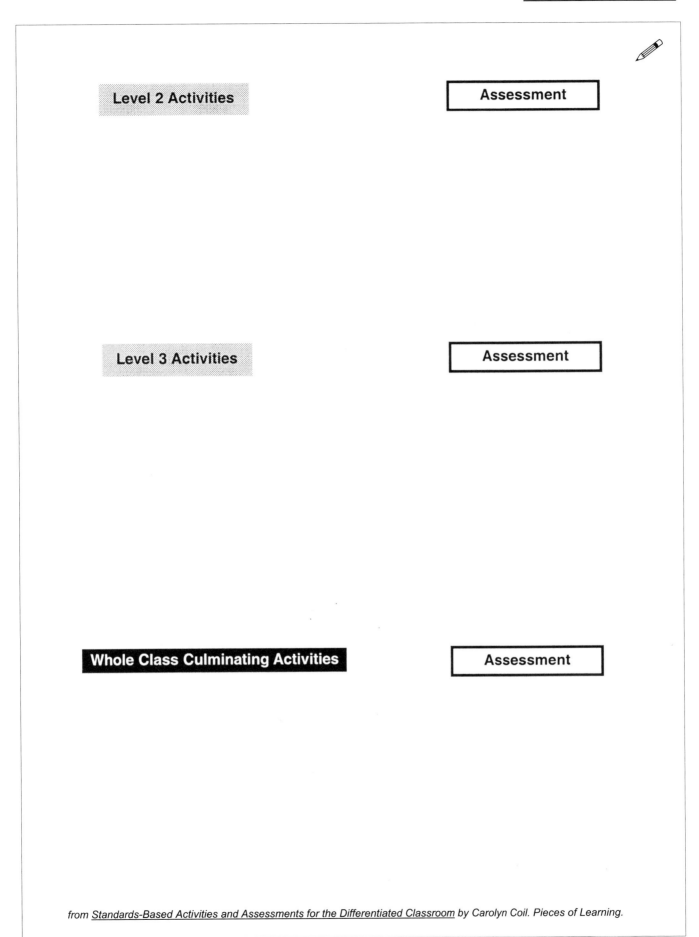

Level 2 Activities

Assessment

Level 3 Activities

Assessment

Whole Class Culminating Activities

Assessment

from Standards-Based Activities and Assessments for the Differentiated Classroom by Carolyn Coil. Pieces of Learning.

Developing a Philosophy of Gifted Education

The Richardson Study, a national study on educating able learners conducted by the Sid W. Richardson Foundation from 1982-1985, recommended that school districts and communities develop a written philosophy for the education of able learners consistent with local goals and values. Below is a reproducible page to use to begin writing your own philosophy of gifted education. Use it with other teachers, parents, and community leaders to develop a gifted philosophy in your school district. A sample philosophy combined from several I have helped to develop is on the next page. Use it as a model and a tool in developing your own.

A Philosophy of Gifted Education

I believe that gifted students:

I believe that a program for gifted students:

Sample Philosophy of Gifted Education *

I believe that gifted students:

1. Have highly individualized needs reflected in high intellectual abilities, unique talents, and differences in learning styles, emotional needs, and social development.

2. Possess potential for independent and critical thinking and benefit from active exploration, questioning, and investigation.

3. Require continuous stimulation and encouragement in the areas of motivation and social interaction necessary to reach their maximum potential.

4. Perform or have the potential to perform at a level far above the norm for their age and grade.

I believe that a program for gifted students:

1. Should meet the needs of gifted students K-12 by serving a variety of types of giftedness.

2. Should emphasize divergent thinking and higher-level thinking skills.

3. Should offer differentiated learning opportunities focusing on acceleration, enrichment, and extension of the grade-level curriculum.

4. Should provide in-depth enrichment in areas of student interest emphasizing research, communication, and study skills.

5. Should provide guidance and counseling services for emotional support and career education.

6. Should provide for community involvement through college classes, dual enrollment, mentor and external programs, resource professionals, etc.

7. Should be funded so that the program can have well-equipped instructional spaces comparable to regular classrooms with qualified instructors who meet with their classes on a regular basis.

8. Should provide a means of regular communication among the gifted and regular classroom teachers and among teachers and parents.

9. Should be incorporated in the regular classroom so that gifted students are not receiving an appropriate education only when they go to the "gifted class."

10. Should adequately challenge all gifted students.

11. Should involve teachers, parents, and students in planning and implementation.

---

* *Developed by Carolyn Coil with several school districts throughout the United States.*

Self-Assessment: Meeting the Needs of Gifted and Talented Students

Teacher Reflection Page

1 = Most of the time   2 = Some of the time   3 = Seldom   4 = Almost never

The curriculum and learning activities in my classroom and/or school meet the needs of gifted and talented learners by:

_____ 1. Presenting advanced content related to broad-based themes.

_____ 2. Integrating several different subject areas.

_____ 3. Allowing for differences in levels and pace of learning.

_____ 4. Encouraging student choices in studying an area of special interest.

_____ 5. Developing independent study, organization, and time management skills.

_____ 6. Developing higher-level thinking skills.

_____ 7. Focusing on open-ended tasks, questions, and answers.

_____ 8. Developing advanced research skills, including skills in evaluating the reliability of both print and Internet sources.

_____ 9. Integrating basic skills with critical and creative thinking skills.

_____ 10. Encouraging the development of new and unique ideas, materials, methods, techniques, products, performances, or processes.

_____ 11. Providing opportunities for and guidance in the development of leadership skills.

_____ 12. Guiding students in the development of social skills, self-confidence, self-motivation, and self-understanding.

_____ 13. Facilitating curriculum compacting, tiered lessons/units, acceleration, and enrichment.

_____ 14. Considering multiple intelligences and a variety of learning styles.

_____ 15. Providing for advanced study with a mentor, business partner, or other resource person.

_____ 16. Including pathways for ascending intellectual demand within the curriculum.

What are your areas of strength in differentiating curriculum for gifted and talented students? (Look at items rated **1** and **2**)

What are your areas of weakness in differentiating curriculum for gifted and talented students? (Look at items rated **3** and **4**)

Reflections

* Gifted students have outstanding abilities in academics, creativity, leadership, and/or the arts. They differ in individual gifts and talents which makes the term **gifted** difficult to define.

* There are a variety of program models and options for gifted students. Use those that will challenge your students to work hard and to achieve excellence.

* There are many strategies for differentiation to use with gifted students in the regular classroom.

* Various forms of grouping gifted and talented students are effective depending on the circumstances and learning outcomes for each student.

* School districts and communities need to start by developing a written Philosophy of Gifted Education and then consider strategies and approaches for implementing it.

NOTES _____

Chapter 12

Dealing With Conflict

Questions to Consider

1. Why is it important to learn how to prevent and manage conflict?

2. What are some of the causes of and outcomes resulting from conflict?

3. What strategies can we use to deal with conflict constructively?

4. What benefits can be derived from teaching students about conflict and conflict resolution?

It was Monday afternoon, and the week had not started well. Mr. Marks, the Assistant Principal, had done nothing all day except deal with students who were in conflict with one another. Several groups of boys had gotten off the buses arguing and fighting, mostly about things that had happened in their neighborhoods over the weekend. Two boys were threatening to have a fight after school because a certain university team had lost a football game! Two girls were fighting over a boyfriend, and another group of students was accusing each other of cheating on a test. It seemed to Mr. Marks that conflicts, potential violence, and hostility were everywhere.

Ms. Gomez and Ms. Dunn listened carefully when the principal explained that there needed to be much more collaboration among teachers during the upcoming school year. Each felt that they would be better off just closing their doors and teaching like they always had. After all, both had seen new ideas come and go. Furthermore, they felt resentful when they learned they were to collaborate with one another and share responsibility for each other's students. Like many other teachers, Ms. Gomez and Ms. Dunn felt some of the internal conflict change inevitably brings. Neither felt very positive about being part of a collaborative team.

Mr. Marks is not alone. While we strive for the goal of having a "safe and orderly environment" in all our schools, often the reality is that teachers and principals spend a great deal of time just trying to prevent and manage conflicts. The reactions of Ms. Gomez and Ms. Dunn are typical, too. Conflict is invariably part of the change process. Most schools are involved in a variety of changes. Typically, some people want change while others wish to maintain the status quo. And even those who favor change may have different points of view. Conflict is inevitable.

For these reasons, the ability to prevent and manage conflicts is one of the major needs of schools today and most likely will be throughout the 21st century. In this chapter, we will look at conflicts and the tools we can use to deal with them in the school setting.

Definition of Conflict

A **conflict** is a **state of tension or disagreement between two or more people, ideas, nations, systems, or communities.** It occurs as a byproduct of our interdependence on one another. People deal with conflict in different ways. Some are conflict avoiders and seek to deny or postpone conflict at all costs. At the other extreme are persons who are always looking for a fight or dispute. Most people fall somewhere between these two extremes.

Causes of Conflict

Several things may cause conflicts. Major causes are:

1. **Scarcity** (or perceived scarcity) of something that more than one person or group wants, such as goods, money, rewards, prizes, privileges, status, advancement, etc. Schools often are faced with conflicts due to scarcity. Students may feel that other students get more privileges or opportunities than they do. Parents complain that their child is not receiving equitable treatment or services. Teachers often feel that certain favored staff members get more than their fair share of scarce resources, citing everything from curricular materials to a duty-free lunch. When there are many wants and needs and not enough resources or rewards, conflict will occur.

2. **Differences in values or opinions** within a given system, such as goals that should be worked for, the direction an organization should go, the rules or laws that should be made, etc. Differences in values and opinions have always been part of the American landscape. In fact, our Founding Fathers shaped our democracy with the knowledge that a free people would have diverse opinions. As our schools become less homogeneous and more culturally diverse, and as society has more and more difficulty agreeing on a common set of values, these differences will cause conflicts in schools. Administrators, students, teachers, various groups of parents, political leaders, and others will express conflicting opinions about the nature and role of the school. This will likely continue to be a source of conflict throughout the 21st century.

3. **Pressure and emotions** experienced by individuals resulting in "explosions" toward one another. Many people experience a great deal of stress and pressure. Usually, most people handle their stress well, but we all go through times when we have more than enough! When pressures mount and emotions boil over, conflict can result. When this happens, the conflict at hand is usually not the underlying problem. It is more likely to be the symptom of other problems.

4. **Personality factors** that make up each person surface when facing the anxieties and problems of life. Some people take an aggressive, unyielding stance when faced with conflict or disagreement. Others are not assertive and expect that others will somehow read their minds. These people get hurt when they discover their needs have not been met. Some people approach conflict with no emotion, others are excessively emotional. These different personalities add to the complexity of conflict resolution.

Conflict: Positive or Negative?

Conflict can have both positive and negative outcomes. Whether the conflict has a positive or negative influence on those involved depends largely upon how the participants handle the conflict. Does it escalate to the point it becomes violent and unmanageable and results in destruction? Or are the dynamics of the situation managed to promote growth and new directions for the participants? Either outcome is possible as a result of a conflict situation.

Positive Outcomes from Conflict Situations

1. Provides drama and adventure.

2. Gives an opportunity to explore differences and hear both sides.

3. Motivates people to engage in problem solving and change the situation.

4. Clears the air and provides both parties with a better understanding of one another.

5. Improves communication and creates new perspectives.

6. Contributes to long term progress if the conflict is resolved.

7. Can be a catalyst for energy and creativity.

Negative Outcomes from Conflict Situations

1. Can cause hurt feelings.

2. Increases anger that can lead to threats, violence, and destruction.

3. Causes emotional and/or communication breakdowns.

4. Person who doesn't like conflict will withdraw and the problem isn't solved.

5. Leads to illnesses caused by stress.

6. May be costly in terms of time, money, and other resources.

7. May result in physical harm or death.

8. Takes emphasis off other things that are more important. For example, settling fights instead of academic learning; bickering rather than collaborating.

Conflict Management and Conflict Resolution

People involved in conflicts can manage them effectively if they learn to trust the other person(s) involved and not let the negative tension that comes from the conflict engulf them. Use the 10 steps listed below as guidelines in resolving and managing the conflicts you face.

10 Steps to Successful Conflict Resolution

1. Establish the appropriate physical environment and personal attitude. Build rapport and avoid blaming the other person.

2. Make sure everyone agrees on what the conflict is really about. Stick to the problem at hand. Do not let personal issues get in the way of conflict resolution.

3. Talk about needs, feelings, and interests instead of opinions or positions of disagreement. Attempt to see the other person's point of view as well as your own.

4. Restate the issues in the conflict so that it is possible to find common ground. Focusing on common problems, interests, or goals often leads to common solutions and areas of agreement.

5. Work on the easiest areas for resolution – the part that seems most likely to be solved – first.

6. Brainstorm possible solutions that address the needs of both sides. Use objective criteria when exploring possible solutions.

7. Have acceptable alternatives in mind to suggest if you don't get exactly what you want.

8. Collaborate on an equitable solution. Attempt to come to agreement on a joint action that is acceptable to all involved.

9. Accommodate face saving for all parties

10. Communicate, communicate, communicate! This is the best tool for resolving any conflict.

RESOLVING CLASSROOM CONFLICTS

As much as possible, allow students to resolve their own problems. Point out and define the problem for your students, and then help them in learning how to resolve the situation. Remove both parties from the group for a specified amount of time if participants cannot resolve a classroom conflict. Use direct intervention if physical harm could come to a student as a result of the conflict situation.

Conflict in the Primary Grades

Prevention is the **KEY** to avoiding conflicts among children in the classroom. It is possible to structure your classroom so that, for the most part, conflict will not occur. Arrange the day so there is a combination of quiet and energetic activities. Make one of the rules of the class "Be kind to others." This covers a multitude of behaviors including any situation that might involve conflict. Review the rules every day, and use the rule whenever a potential conflict arises. Constantly **model** the *"Be kind to others"* rule and point out to the students when someone is being kind. If you model and reinforce good behavior, it will happen. Before breaking into small groups for any activity with movement or any type of give and take among children, discuss limits, classroom rules, and sharing.

Most conflict in the early grades has to do with learning to share and taking turns. Watch for children who are doing these things and give them positive feedback. Praise students when they are doing something that follows the rule of being kind. Some primary-aged children can be talked to at their chronological age level, but others have the social development of two or three-year-olds, and their reasoning skills may not yet be developed. The teacher must consider developmental age, not chronological age, when dealing with conflicts among young children. Meet them where they are, and bring them forward.

Conflict and Older Students

Like younger students, the key to avoiding many conflicts is prevention. At the beginning of the school year when you review the class rules, include rules that will reduce the possibility of conflicts developing in your classroom. Often, verbal taunts and accusations lead to greater conflicts among students. Therefore, create some of your rules as guidelines for verbal exchanges between students. Often your students can collaborate with you in making classroom rules that result in fewer situations of conflict. State these rules and guidelines in a positive way. Some examples, which were all developed with the help of students, are:

- ❑ Use words that will build others up when talking to or about them.
- ❑ Talk in a positive way when you have comments to make about others.
- ❑ If something is bothering you about another person, talk to that person directly about the problem. Ask for help in solving the problem rather than making accusations.
- ❑ Give compliments, not criticisms, to others.
- ❑ If you disagree with someone, sometimes it is better to just walk away.

Rivalries Between Students

Beginning in the intermediate grades and through adolescence, rivalries between groups of students seem to develop quickly. These begin with one child deciding she/he does not like another. He or she then tries to pull others to his or her side. This type of situation can escalate quickly. If you are aware that this is taking place, action on your part can squelch the conflict almost immediately. Take these steps:

- ❑ Gather all involved.
- ❑ Ask each person to tell his/her version about what is occurring.
- ❑ When one person is talking, no one is to interrupt.
- ❑ Analyze the underlying causes of the conflict.
- ❑ Mentally pinpoint ringleaders.
- ❑ Verbalize the situation as you see it.
- ❑ Make a suggestion of what you would do.
- ❑ Ask for other suggestions to help solve the problem.
- ❑ Come to consensus.

When you lead students through this problem solving method, explain that the reason you are guiding them is because you care about all of them and you are concerned. Establish a level of trust between teacher and students. It needs to be present for this method to work successfully.

CONFLICTS AND VIOLENCE ON THE OUTSIDE

Many students come to school with "little storm clouds" hanging over their heads. They bring to school the troubles and problems they face during the 18 hours of the day when they are not in school. They often struggle with a negative attitude that they bring into the classroom from their homes or neighborhoods. Some may be gang members involved in gang violence or retaliation. If you are a good listener, you can often gain a great deal of information about what is going on outside school. Conflicts that begin in the neighborhood or on the bus sometimes escalate during the school day. Other disagreements that start at school continue as the students go home in the afternoon. When you become aware this is happening, discuss it with the students involved.

Parents and Conflict

Keep a record of specific behaviors and conflict situations for each child. If this type of attitude continues in spite of teacher interventions and problem solving, call the parents. Parents sometimes deny that there is conflict at home. Even when we, as teachers, know that this is not the case, our position is not to fix their home. We can only deal with what is happening at school. What we're teaching students about getting along with others and about correct behavior and relationships with others may be directly opposite of what they experience at home and in their neighborhoods. So the home and the school send mixed messages. Our values in the school are not necessarily the same values the parents have. Consider these scenarios.

> *Some students were using bad language. When the teacher remarked, "We don't use ugly words when we talk to one another," one student replied, "My mama says those words hundreds of times every day."*
>
> *One student was seen hitting another student. When the teacher said, "We don't hit other people," this boy responded, "I hit my Dad sometimes. My Dad hits my Mom, and he hits me, so I hit him back."*

As these two examples illustrate, violence and conflict in both word and deed are commonplace in some homes. For some of our students, this is considered the behavioral norm. When confronted by such attitudes teachers need to show students there is another way to manage conflicts. This does not mean pointing out to students why and how their parents are wrong. It does mean showing by example in the classroom and school setting how to resolve conflicts without violence. Use active listening skills and problem solving skills so that all points of view are heard and a number of options for resolving the conflict are considered.

Conflict in our Culture

Remember that conflict often results from a difference in values and opinions. The values we teach in school about managing conflict in nonviolent ways is a very different message from the messages given to children in the pop culture, on television, in videos and computer games, on the streets, and sometimes in their own homes.

> *The students were loud as they filed into first period class on the day after the shooting. Television crews were all over town, and it seemed that the killing of a prominent citizen was big news. One student said to his teacher, "My uncle was killed last month, and I didn't see no television cameras here then. He and this other guy was fighting over something and the gun went off and he was dead."*

For some of our students, conflict and violence is a way of life. They see it personally every day. For these students, the role model is one of using violence to resolve conflicts. Many more of our students are exposed to violence indirectly through the media and technological games and toys.

Since September 11, 2001, all of us are more aware of the way random killings may be used by others. The ongoing War on Terrorism affects our attitudes about dealing with conflict at home and at school. Living with conflict or the threat of conflict is part of everyday life.

One way to deal with this with student attitudes about conflict and conflict among students is to include lessons about conflict in your ongoing curriculum. Use the Tools on the following pages. Begin with the **Student Questionnaire**. This will give you and your students insights about how they personally react in situations of conflict with a variety of people. This is a good activity to use in helping students discover the personal nature of conflict. Their reactions to situations most often depend upon with whom they have conflict.

You will find a **Lesson Plan for Conflict Management** that focuses students on the concept of conflict in a less personal way. There are also samples of a thematic web, **ILP™**, and **Questivities**™ to use in a more in-depth study of **Conflict**.

Student Questionnaire

Name _____   Grade _____

When you have a conflict or a disagreement with someone, how do you react? You may react differently depending upon the person. Listed below you will find several types of people with whom you live, work, and play.

For each of these people, complete the sentence: "When I disagree with or have a conflict with this person, I usually . . ."

1. Parent:

2. Brother or sister:

3. Step-parent:

4. Grandparent:

5. Teacher:

6. Classmate I don't like:

7. Person who has called me names:

8. Someone of a different racial or ethnic group:

9. Someone who hangs out in a different crowd than I do:

10. My best friend:

Conflict Management Lesson Plan *

1. Definition

On newsprint or the board, write the word **conflict**. Brainstorm with the students what they think it means. Write their ideas.

2. Compare and Contrast the Shades of Meaning

Compare and contrast the definitions the students have generated plus any of your own that have not been mentioned. Discuss similarities and differences in the meanings.

3. Making a Continuum (Large and Small Groups)

Draw a horizontal line the full length of the board. Write *Less Severe* at the end of the line to the left and *Most Severe* at the end of the line on the right. Divide the students into six small groups. Ask each group to write each of the definitions where they think they should be placed on the continuum. Discuss the placements, having students from the different groups write the placement on the board.

4. Categorizing Types of Conflict (Small Groups)

Assign each small group a type of conflict. Have each group prepare and then perform a skit illustrating their type of conflict. Suggestions for types of conflict:

- *Conflict within yourself*

- *Conflict among people in the same family*

- *Conflict among people in the same school or neighborhood*

- *Conflict among people in the same country*

- *Conflict among countries*

- *Conflict among ideas*

5. Discussion (Large Group)

Are conflicts ever worth having?

When are they detrimental?

When are they helpful?

* Adapted from *Motivating Underachievers* by Carolyn Coil. Pieces of Learning. Marion, IL

Learning Modality

- Verbal

Learning Style

- Abstract Random

Taxonomy Level

- Application

Multiple Intelligence

- Interpersonal

- Verbal/Linguistic

Assessment Mini-Rubric

- Clarity of conflict
- Resolution of conflict
- Flow of presentation
- Preparation

Conflict Questivities™

Project Activity

Role play a conflict between two students or between a child and a parent. make sure the conflict comes to some resolution.

Project Question

- What would a typical conflict be between two students or among children and parents?

Questivities™ Thinking Questions

1. List typical conflicts between students or among children and parents.

2. Compare/contrast a conflict with a parent and a conflict with another student.

3. How would you feel if you had an opinion about a controversial issue and all of your friends had the opposite opinion?

4. Would you rather avoid a conflict or resolve the problem even though it would cause an argument?

5. Why are so many conflicts settled with violence?

6. How can conflicts be resolved so that both sides are satisfied?

7. What would happen if conflicts in school were never solved? If there were no conflicts in your school?

Active Question

Make a list of questions your mom or dad might ask you concerning an issue about which you disagree.

> **Directions:** Answer the Questivities™ Thinking Questions and the Active Question before doing the Project Activity.

Conflict in Schools

Teacher Reflection Page

Think about the conflicts you have faced in the last few months. Review the information found on the previous pages to help you reflect on these questions.

1. Think about a conflict that you have had with another staff member at your school. Consider the following issues:

- What was the major cause of the conflict?
- Did both parties agree on what the conflict was really about?
- Was the conflict resolved to your satisfaction?
- What were some unspoken issues in this conflict?
- Was trust and rapport present?
- Was one person in a more powerful negotiating position?
- How did this affect the outcome or resolution of the conflict?
- What were the positive outcomes of the conflict? Negative outcomes?
- What would you do differently if a similar situation occurs again?

2. Consider a conflict you have had with a parent. Think about the following:

- What common goals and interests did you and the parent have?
- What emotional or personal attitudes made it difficult to resolve this conflict?
- What alternatives did you offer that would meet the needs of both persons?
- Would it have been helpful to have involved more people? Fewer people? Why?
- In which areas was there good communication?
- In which areas did communication tend to break down?

3. List several conflicts involving students. Choose one and then consider . . .

- What was the cause of the conflict?
- What positive outcomes occurred?
- What negative outcomes occurred?
- What strategies did you use in solving the conflict?
- What other strategies could you have used?

4. How do conflicts from the outside world affect your students and your classroom? How can you handle this?

5. What are some of your strengths in resolving or managing conflicts? What are some of your weaknesses?

6. What would you like to change about your conflict management style and strategies?

Conflict

Make a collage of conflict stories from newspapers or magazines.

Diagram a historic conflict from causes to resolution.

Role play a conflict between a child and a parent.

Pantomime how to solve conflicts without violence.

Make a video showing how conflicts can be solved without violence.

Read a book and make a web of the conflicts in the story.

View 10 different TV shows. List all of the conflicts you see.

Make a compare/contrast chart comparing conflicts in any two short stories.

Create a computerized data base of historic conflicts which led to war.

Demonstrate similarities and differences between sports and conflicts.

Write a letter to someone you are having a conflict with. Explain your solution to the conflict.

Draw a series of cartoons showing different kinds of conflict.

INDIVIDUAL LESSON PLAN - CONFLICT

ACTIVITIES - STUDENT CHOICES

Visual

1. Make a compare/contrast chart comparing conflicts in any two short stories.
2. Diagram a historic conflict from causes to resolution.
3. Draw a series of cartoons showing different kinds of conflict.

Verbal

7. Read a a book and make a mindmap of the conflicts in the story.
8. Role play a conflict between a child and a parent.
9. Write a letter to someone you are having a conflict with. Explain your solution to the conflict.

Kinesthetic

4. Make a collage of conflict stories from newspapers or magazines.
5. Pantomime how to solve conflicts without violence.
6. Demonstrate similarities and differences between sports and conflicts.

Technological

10. View 10 different TV shows. List all of the conflicts you see.
11. Make a video showing how conflicts can be solved without violence.
12. Create a computerized data base of historic conflicts which led to war.

Required Activities Teacher's Choice

1. Generate a list of class rules & procedures that will help prevent conflicts.
2. Use a problem solving method to identify & solve an existing classroom conflict.
3. Do Conflict Management Lesson. (from page 196)

Product/Performance Required

1. Class list of rules and procedures.
2. Mutually agreed upon solution.
3. Continuum of conflicts

Assessment Required Activities

1. List agreed upon by all class members; group participation
2. Problem was identified; criteria generated and used in problem solving
3. Logical reasons for placement of types of conflicts on continuum.

Standards

Optional Student-Parent Cooperative Activity

Using a problem solving method to identify and solve an existing conflict between student and parent.

Student Choices in Ways to Learn

Visual
_____
_____

Kinesthetic
_____
_____

Verbal
_____
_____

Technological
_____
_____

Product/Performance Student Choice

Due Date Student Choice

Reflections

* The ability to prevent and manage conflict is a major need for anyone who interacts with others in some way.

* Conflict has many causes and can have both positive and negative outcomes.

* Prevention, problem solving, and direct intervention are three strategies for dealing with conflicts among students.

* Lessons about conflict and conflict resolution can help students learn to handle conflicts effectively.

Notes _____

Chapter 13

Parent/Teacher Collaboration

Questions to Consider

1. What are the essential skills in communicating with parents?

2. Why are trust and respect so important in building collaborative relationships?

3. What are the purposes of Parent/Teacher conferences? How can we structure them for optimum benefit?

4. How can teachers develop effective strategies to involve parents?

5. Why is parent/teacher collaboration important?

Ms. Fenwick breathed a sigh of relief. Her students were gone for the day and she could take a moment to relax. She smiled as she thought about the exuberance of the six and seven-year-olds she teaches every day. She tried to remember her own childhood and thought back to her own first grade class. "The thing I remember most," she decided, "was trying to write the letters of the alphabet so that each looked perfect on my paper. I would get so frustrated when my attempts didn't look as good as the teacher's examples! I don't know if any of my students even care about things like that."

Growing up in the 21st century isn't the same as growing up in the 1970s, 1980s or 1990s. Close your eyes and take a few moments to reflect on some memories from your own childhood. Then in the left-hand column of the chart on the next page, list outstanding things, events, places, and activities you can remember from your own childhood. Next, in the right-hand column, list typical events, places, and activities an average child in your class might experience today. As you look at the two lists, what conclusions can you make? What things have changed?

© Carolyn Coil

Memories from My Childhood	Typical Activities of Children Today

Observations

Changes

Conclusions

Like teachers, parents are also feeling the effects of the tremendous changes the 21st century has brought. Parents look at everything going on in the world, in their community, and even within the school and may see vast differences from their childhood experiences. Often this is a good way to begin establishing a collaborative relationship with parents, for many parents and teachers look at the world through similar generational eyes.

If you are 15 or more years older or younger than the parents of your students, talk about differences between your childhood memories and theirs, and then reflect on further differences in their child's experiences.

"Collaboration" is one of the buzz words in education, but we must go further than merely repeating the appropriate words. We must sincerely want parent participation and input into their child's education. Parents need to be involved in the day-in and day-out activities of the school. The more they are involved, the more they will understand about the world their child lives in for a good portion of each day. The more parents are involved, the more they will appreciate, understand, and support the schools.

Parents and teachers have complementary but separate roles that together can nurture students' growth. Parents can provide valuable information about their child's behavior, educational concerns, strengths, weaknesses, and how to manage their child. Additionally, recent research has shown that parental attitude and encouragement can affect school success at least as much as a child's IQ. Often the difference between children who do well in school and those who do not relates to their parents' attitudes about school. In other words, positive parental involvement enables children to achieve better and learn more.

Parents and No Child Left Behind (NCLB)

The *No Child Left Behind* law encourages parental involvement and communication between home and school. It requires that every school make adequate yearly progress (AYP) in improving student achievement. This includes all schools and all children. Additionally, it specifies that both the state and individual school districts give parents easy-to-read report cards on schools and school districts. These report cards must contain information on student achievement and show achievement gaps among different sub groups of students. They must identify schools that need improvement, show high school graduation rates, and delineate teacher qualifications.

Low-performing schools receiving federal funds must make improvements. If they do not improve, parents have the option of transferring their child to a higher-performing public school in the same district. They can also receive supplemental educational services such as tutoring, after-school programs, or remedial classes that are paid for by the school district.

Because this law is so important to schools, and because it involves and includes parents in many of its provisions, it can be an important vehicle in parent/teacher collaboration.

Productive Communication between Parents and Teachers

The essentials in any productive communication involve skills in both speaking and listening.

As good communicators, teachers must be sure that they express their ideas and concerns clearly and that parents understand them. State problems as simply as possible, and do not ignore or avoid them. It is very important for parents to understand when there are problems and why these problems are occurring. Therefore, it is essential to state a child's behavior in real terms that parents can understand and with which they can identify. Be specific. Don't use educational jargon and say, *"We're seeing some signs of aggression in Jeremy."* Instead, explain the problem: *"Jeremy has been in three fights during recess this week."*

As good listeners, teachers must be sure they listen carefully so they will really understand the parents' point of view. Concentrate on what the other person is saying. Don't be thinking about the next statement you will make and miss what the parent is saying. Too often what passes for listening is arguing mentally as the other person makes his or her points!

People often communicate more nonverbally than they do verbally. Be aware of the parent's nonverbal language as well as what he or she is saying in words. Also be aware that different cultures have different types of nonverbal communication and customs. Eye contact or specific gestures may mean one thing to you and something completely different to a parent from a different ethnic or cultural background.

On the next two pages you will find

- **Cultural Characteristics that May Affect Parent/Teacher Communications**

    This general list of characteristics may help you as you interact with parents from different cultural backgrounds. Use it to help in understanding why a parent is acting in a certain way. However, do not use it to stereotype any cultural group.

- **Key Elements of Good Communication**

This Reflection Page will help you think in more depth about the skills of good listening and good speaking and how both of these affect your interactions with parents.

Cultural Characteristics That May Affect Parent/Teacher Communication

African American

- Personal questions at first meeting may be seen as intrusive
- Verbally inventive with semantic inversions ("bad" may mean "good")
- Indirect eye contact when listening; direct eye contact when speaking
- Emotional intensity and expression during conversation
- Physically expressive with gestures and body language
- Deep sense of cultural history
- Value equality of opportunity

Hispanic

- Physical closeness during conversation (12 to 18 inches apart)
- Flexible sense of time
- Extended family important
- Hissing to get attention is acceptable, especially from males
- Sustained direct eye contact may be interpreted as a challenge to authority
- Eye contact is important during conversation
- Emotional intensity in conversation
- Value hard work

Asian American

- Reserved with a respect for silence and control
- Orientation toward privacy with disdain for public reprimand
- Drop eyes to show respect
- Laugh when embarrassed (particularly true for females)
- May take offense at the use of nicknames or first names only
- Maybe considered inappropriate to shake hands with a person of the opposite sex
- Parent/teacher conference may be regarded as a meeting where bad news will be given
- Value formal education

Anglo American

- Respect direct and polite conversation
- Nuclear family more important than extended family
- Preference for promptness
- Emotional restraint in public behavior
- Competitive and individualistic
- May want comparisons of own child to others in class
- Value grades and points earned by child

Key Elements of Good Communication

Teacher Reflection Page

Take a few minutes to jot down what you feel are the key elements of good listening and of good speaking. Then discuss your ideas with several other teachers. As a group list these elements and share this information at a staff meeting.

List 5 important elements of good listening:

1.

2.

3.

4.

5.

List 5 important elements of good speaking:

1.

2.

3.

4.

5.

Implications in working with parents:

Developing Trust and Respect Between School and Home

Many teachers look upon the idea of parent/teacher collaboration as a source of stress and anxiety. Teachers may be reluctant to share information about a student or may be afraid of criticism or of not living up to parental expectations.

Parents also may be reluctant to enter into a collaborative relationship with the school. They may have negative attitudes toward teachers based on their own childhood school experiences. They may previously have had unpleasant experiences with teachers and other school personnel when they were trying to help their child. Negative feelings may also stem from problems they have had with their child, of feelings of failure, blame or guilt for something that has gone wrong at home or school.

The critical factors of trust and rapport are repeatedly the most important things in a parent/teacher relationship. Parents can see the same issues in either a positive or a negative way. It is the trust factor that makes the difference.

Things for Teachers to Remember About Parents

There may be several causes for parents' behaviors and attitudes toward you. Consider the following factors when you wonder why parents are acting in a certain way:

- ❑ Their childhood experiences
- ❑ Their experiences with teachers and schools
- ❑ Their relationships with their parents
- ❑ Their fears and insecurities
- ❑ Their hopes and expectations
- ❑ Their careers and work
- ❑ Their relationship with their spouse
- ❑ Their self-confidence or lack of it
- ❑ Their current emotional status
- ❑ Their experiences with other children and the school
- ❑ Their cultural, ethnic, or linguistic background

An essential element in building an atmosphere conducive to effective parent/teacher collaboration is having a *Circle of Respect* that involves students, parents, and their teachers. This means that all parties truly respect and trust one another. They have the confidence that each is doing his or her best to work toward excellence in the learning process. A break anywhere in this circle usually results in a breakdown in student performance.

Unfortunately, teachers, parents, and students do not always promote this sense of mutual respect. Do your best to keep the *Circle of Respect* intact at your school. If it is broken, see what you can do to rebuild the mutual respect of all those in your school who are involved in the education of children.

Planning the Parent/Teacher Conference

One way to establish a collaborative relationship with parents is through the Parent/Teacher Conference. This provides a structured opportunity for parents and teachers to discuss mutual concerns and to work together. Successful Parent/Teacher Conferences require planning. Part of this planning is to realize that sometimes participants may come to the conference with hidden agendas. It is important to consider this before planning the conference itself.

Hidden agendas and fears often break the *Circle of Respect*. Either a parent or a teacher may come to the conference with a hidden agenda. These agendas exist for many reasons. Sometimes people don't understand their own feelings very well, or they may be embarrassed to admit how they really feel. There may be pressure from a third party or situation. Any of these factors may create hidden agendas. Some hidden agendas that may be present in the Parent/Teacher Conference are:

- Need to assert power and control

- Need to feel needed

- Desire to impress the others at the conference

- Protection of a loved one

- Feelings of inadequacy

- Need to appease the other parent, especially if that parent is not at the conference

- Desire for help or intervention but not knowing how to ask

- Need to impress colleagues or superiors

- Negative feelings about a certain group or a certain type of parents/teachers

Providing a structure and using it to plan ahead is an important strategy to use in Parent/Teacher Conferences. Because the input of parents and collaboration between parents and teachers is so valuable, teachers need to approach the conference in a way that ensures that the greatest benefit can be derived from it.

Do this by planning thoroughly for the conference, using a checklist of important points. This structure enables teachers to review the items that need to be prepared ahead of time, spot check for good communication during the conference, and schedule follow-up details after the conference is over. This structure provides a concrete method to make sure you are really doing what your good intentions want to do in the first place!

The **Parent/Teacher Conference Checklist** found on pages 211-212 provides a structure for conferences and simplifies all of the little details that are often overlooked because of a teacher's busy schedule. Use this tool as you plan your Parent/Teacher Conferences.

How to Gather Relevant Documentation

There are a number of different ways to document student behavior and parent contacts. Here are some suggestions:

- ❑ Use a small notebook using one page for each student.
- ❑ Keep a file of index cards with one card for each student.
- ❑ Utilize a folder that allows you to insert as many pages as are needed for each student as well as work samples.
- ❑ Devise a standard form for all phone contacts and conferences that can be used for all students.
- ❑ Create a computerized database for each student with dates, times, major items discussed, et.
- ❑ Have students keep a log of daily or weekly work. Sign or initial it regularly.
- ❑ Print out any e-mail correspondence with parents and file it with other parent contact information

- Be aware that parents are entitled to see any documentation in their child's cumulative record folder that goes from one grade to the next. According to the **Family Educational Rights and Privacy Act of 1974 and as amended in 1988, 1993, and 2000 (PL 93-380)** *parents have "the right to inspect and review any and all official records, files, and data directly related to their children, including all material that is incorporated into each student's cumulative record folder...specifically including, but not necessarily limited to, identifying data, academic work completed, level of achievement, attendance data, scores on standardized intelligence, aptitude and psychological tests, interest inventory results, health data, family background information, teacher or counselor ratings and observations, and verified reports of serious or recurrent behavior patterns."*

  This law also requires limited parental access to standardized tests because test booklets are considered educational records. As the impact of *NCLB* grows, school districts may receive more and more requests from parents to see the high-stakes tests.

Parent/Teacher Conference Checklist

Pre-Conference Planning

❑ 1. Verify meeting place, time and length, making sure this is convenient for the parent.

❑ 2. Communicate conference purpose.
   Purposes may include:
   Reporting on specific academic, behavioral or affective
   Strengths/weaknesses
   Information gathering
   Program planning
   Problem solving

❑ 3. Be familiar with the child.
   Study information in the child's file.
   Know relevant data about tests, health, strengths, weaknesses.
   Obtain information from other teachers as appropriate.
   Gather work samples and other documentation.
   Make sure you include positive aspects of a child's performance.

❑ 4. Plan agenda.
   List conference purpose.
   List items of concern to you.
   Leave space to add parent concerns to the agenda.

❑ 5. Arrange the physical environment.
   Privacy
   No distractions
   Comfortable temperature
   Seating arrangements
   No physical barriers between participants
   All participants should have a seat which indicates equal power.
   Circular or square arrangement works best
   Use adult-sized chairs if possible - if parents must sit in small chairs, teacher should do the same.
   Materials and work samples available

The Conference

_____ 1. Welcome the parent.

> Greet the parent at the school office when possible.
> Be on time and have a contingency plan for emergency delays.
> Establish rapport through friendly comments and positive non-verbals.

_____ 2. Introduce agenda, purpose, and conference timetable.

> Allow for parent additions.
> Give option for note taking.

_____ 3. Listen and share information.

> Restate the purpose of the conference.
> Follow agenda, giving time for parent input at every stage.
> Communicate specific information.
> Stick to the issues.
> Ask for questions.

_____ 4. Summarize conference content and decisions.

_____ 5. Set dates and/or sequence of events for follow-up.

_____ 6. End in a positive way.

Post-Conference

_____ 1. Document and file conference agenda and notes.

_____ 2. Prepare a conference summary for parents.

_____ 3. Review with the child if appropriate.

_____ 4. Share information with other school personnel if appropriate.

(Note: Don't turn this into gossip about the child or the parent. What is said in the conference is not appropriate for staff room talk.)

_____ 5. Establish time line for implementing conference follow-up.

_____ 6. Mark calendar and/or plan book for doing follow-up.

_____ 7. Complete any other documentation required by your school or district.

Complexity of Parenting

Not only has family structure changed during the past 30 years, but also the skills needed to meet the demands placed on parents have grown more and more complex. Parents must fill numerous roles with their children while they are balancing a multitude of other demands. Many parents are simply overwhelmed at the task that confronts them. Some have all but given up.

Parents legitimately want to have a voice in the education of their children. When teachers and parents view the educational process as a collaborative effort, we need strategies that enhance the child's growth and promotes more effective learning.

Other Ways to Communicate With Parents

Because teachers are so busy, good *intentions* about collaborating with parents are not enough. It simply will not happen unless you schedule it. Make a time for this to happen. Choose any of the following methods to communicate with the parents of your students.

1. Make positive phone calls to parents.

This is one of the most effective techniques. A brief update about the student is all that is needed. If a habit of positive phone calls is established, the lines of communication will be open when there is a problem. In a positive phone call:

- Describe the student's positive behavior

- Describe how you feel about the behavior

- Ask the parent to share what you have said with their child

If at all possible, don't make the first contact you have with the parent a negative one.

2. Send notes, cards, and letters to parents.

A positive note consists of a few lines written to the parent that tell something good about their child. Keep a file of ready-to-use notes. Plan to send home a specific number each week. Send preprinted messages, memos, and academic awards. Send home a birthday card on each student's birthday. Get well cards are important when a student is sick for more than a few days. Be sure to acknowledge parent help with a thank you note.

3. Use all types of home/school communication techniques.

Have students keep a daily journal which goes back and forth between home and school. Send student work home each Friday in a special envelope for parents. Send home a weekly newsletter telling about events in your classroom and areas of study. Publicize school activities in the newspaper.

4. Use new technologies.

Voice mail, homework hotlines, e-mail, faxes, videos of student work, instant messages, teleconferencing, class and school web sites, and other new technologies are helpful tools in communicating with parents. The Information Age can also be called the Communication Age. Take advantage of it!

5. Provide information about how to help children at home.

Share rubrics with parents and explain how they work. Give guidelines about how much help is appropriate and how to help their child without doing his/her work.

Parents and Homework

Homework has the potential to be the most consistent day-to-day contact you have with parents, particularly in the upper grades. Yet parents complain that this is the greatest cause of conflict between them and their children. On the other hand, teachers complain that students don't complete assignments, and parents won't see that they do. Often, parents don't understand why homework is given, when it will be given, how it is expected to be done, or what they can do to help.

Make sure you have a homework policy that states the expectations of students, parents, and the teacher. Parents need to be kept informed about class work, upcoming tests and projects, and ways they can help their child to study. Provide parents with suggestions for assisting with homework and information about helping their child develop good study skills. ***Becoming an Achiever*** (Pieces of Learning, 2004) a workbook for students that offers many study skills suggestions. Distribute the reproducible message about Homework written in both Spanish and English found at the end of this chapter.

Parent Involvement

Parental involvement in schools usually begins with principals and teachers reaching out to parents and other family members. Each school and each teacher seem to discover the best ways for working with the parents of their students. Below are several suggestions you may want to consider as you develop effective strategies to involve parents in the educational process.

1. Encourage parents to complete one of the **Student Choice Learning Activities** from the **Individual Lesson Plan™ (ILP)** format with their child. These learning activities and projects should involve parents with their children in an enjoyable and creative way. Record the activity in the space on the **ILP™** that indicates *Optional Student Parent Cooperative Activity*.

2. Be a resource for parents. Keep a list of places to visit, books to read, activities to do with your child, etc. to share with parents as needed. Organize family field trips and excursions. Many families do not take advantage of cultural opportunities that are close at hand. Organize a trip for students and their parents on a Saturday or a holiday. At the end of the day, distribute a list of other opportunities they could take advantage of.

3. Be innovative in thinking about ways to involve parents in your school or classroom. Have special nights for parents where students demonstrate what they are learning. Create a museum of student work and display it for parents. Encourage parents to attend student performances.

4. If feasible, visit the homes of your students. During the visit, discuss school and family issues. A visit to a student's home establishes personal relationships among all of the adults who are from different segments of the child's world. Sometimes a visit can be the impetus for starting a neighborhood group that meets periodically to work on ways to help their children in school.

5. Schedule student-led conferences. Have students explain their work and demonstrate their learning to parents. Have them use work samples to show what they know and what they need to work on. This helps parents understand what their child is doing at school in a tangible way.

6. Distribute informational newsletters to individual parents or to parent groups. Use them at parent meetings, parent/teacher conferences, or as articles in class or school newsletters. They can be a guide to assist you in discussing ways parents can help their children in many aspects of life.

Homework: The Home/School Connection

Homework provides the major intersection and connection between home and school. Most kids have homework they are supposed to do, and this provides the best ongoing opportunity for parents to share in their child's life in school. As every parent knows, homework can also be the biggest battleground between parents and children. Most of us want to avoid the homework wars yet let our children know that we think homework is important. We want them to understand that learning at home while reading and while doing homework is an extension of learning at school.

A number of guidelines regarding homework are below. Read through them and decide which might work best in your household and with your children.

- Set a study time each afternoon or evening when everyone in the house reads and studies. Schedules can get very crowded with activities and socializing, so it is important to establish this time early on.

- Set a reasonable limit on how much time should be spent on homework. Sometimes your child may spend too many hours studying! The teacher should be contacted if you think the amount of homework is extreme.

- Make one area of the house the study and reading area. Have all necessary supplies in this place. These may include books, dictionaries, a computer, paper, pencils, pens, markers, crayons, rulers, etc.

- Take advantage of the public library, especially if you don't have lots of books or a computer in your home. There is a wealth of information in every library and it is there free for you to use!

- Make sure you monitor your children frequently while they are doing homework. Be especially aware of what your child is doing if you have a home computer and access to the Internet. Consider the Internet as a source of information, but also as a way your child can be contacted by anyone in the outside world!

- Homework sometimes is best done at a location near the rest of the family. Kids don't feel isolated or exiled and parents can keep an eye on homework and computer usage. If your child prefers his or her own room as the place to do homework, don't allow access to the Internet there. Whatever the location, the homework area should be reasonably quiet, well lit and the TV should not be on.

from Practical Tips for Parents by Carolyn Coil. Pieces of Learning.

La tarea: la conexión entre el hogar y la escuela

La tarea provee la mayor conección entre el hogar y la escuela. La mayoría de los niños tienen tarea diaria, esto se presta para que los padres puedan compartir con el niño. sus experiencias colegiales. Como padres, sabemos que la tarea también puede ser un gran campo de batalla entre los padres y los niños. La mayoría de nosotros queremos evitar las guerras que producen las tareas, pero, sin embargo, siempre damos mucha énfasis en la importancia de la tarea. Nosotros queremos que nuestros niños comprendan que el aprendizaje en la casa mientras hacen sus tareas es una extensión del aprendizaje en la escuela .

Las siguientes son normas que tienen que ver con el tema de la tarea. Lean y decidan cuáles de estas normas funcionan en su hogar y con sus niños.

- Establezca una hora de estudio por la tarde o por la noche, cuando todos en el hogar lean y estudien. Nuestras agendas pueden llenarse con un sinnúmero de actividades, por lo tanto debemos establecer este tiempo antes de comprometer nuestro tiempo.

- Establezca un límite razonable en cuanto al tiempo que va a dedicar a las tareas. A veces los niZos pasan muchas horas estudiando. Si usted cree que la cantidad de tarea es demasiada, debe de comunicárse con la profesora y hablar de este tema.

- Designe una área de estudio y tenga todos los materiales necesarios en ese lugar. Esto puede incluir enciclopedias, diccionarios, una computadora, papel, lápices, bolígrafos, crayolas, reglas, etc.

- Aprovéchese de la gran oportunidad que le ofrece su biblioteca pública, especialmente si usted en su hogar no posee muchos libros informativos o una computadora. Las bibliotecas públicas poseen una extensa línea informativa gratis que está al alcance de todos.

- Asegúrese de que supervisa frecuentemente a sus niño.s mientras están haciendo la tarea. Esté bien segura de lo que su niño. está haciendo, especialmente si usted tiene una computadora con acceso al Internet. Considere el Internet como un recurso informativo pero también puede ser un contacto directo con el mundo exterior.

from Practical Tips for Parents by Carolyn Coil. Pieces of Learning.

Reflections

* Parent/teacher collaboration involves skills in both speaking and listening, essential elements in productive communication.

* Two important elements in developing collaborative relationships between parents and teachers are trust and respect. Build this through understanding cultural and generational differences and knowing possible fears and hidden agendas parents may have.

* The Parent/Teacher Conference provides a structured opportunity for parents and teachers to discuss mutual concerns and to work together.

* Teachers must plan, schedule, and use a variety of ways to communicate with parents and involve them in schools..

* All parents need our support and assistance in order to fulfill their parenting role, just as schools need parents to help as their children learn. Be a true partner to the parents of your students!

Chapter 14

Technology - A 21st Century Teaching Tool

Questions to Consider

1. What are examples of rapid technological change that you have experienced?

2. How are new technologies impacting teaching and learning in the 21st century?

3. What are educational applications for technology?

4. What roles do teachers have in a "high tech" educational environment?

5. How can we deal with differences among students, teachers, schools and school districts in terms of computer literacy and knowledge computer access, and/or computer hardware and software?

When I am with my "90 something" father, he is a constant reminder of how much has changed in just one person's lifetime. My dad was born in 1913, before the start of World War I. He remembers electricity and telephone lines before they were commonplace in people's homes. He saw the first mass-produced cars and owned a Model A and a Model T Ford.

He remembers Lindbergh's flight across the Atlantic and tells about running outside when he heard a plane in the sky because this was such an unusual phenomenon. He lived in a time when a telegram came to deliver bad news and when people only made a long distance phone call in an emergency. He bought his first TV in the early 1950s, black and white with a 10" screen that appeared to weigh 100 pounds! He has used a manual typewriter all his life and says he sees no reason to change now. I hope they keep manufacturing typewriter ribbons!

My parents don't have a personal computer, a digital camera, or a Palm Pilot. They've never sent an e-mail message, surfed the Internet, or purchased anything online. They do have a VCR, a microwave oven, a color TV, a cell phone, and a brand new car. My dad is a master at using the remote control and can "channel surf" as quickly as anyone I know!

Dad in the 1930s

In many ways, my parents remind me of how schools have embraced technology. We've done something with it, but for the most part we go on functioning just like we have always done.

The world has changed from the Industrial Age to the Information Age. This change is just as significant as the change that the Renaissance brought to the world over 500 years ago but is at a much more rapid pace. Imagine being a teacher of calligraphy to a group of scribes during the Renaissance at the time Gutenberg invented the printing press. You may have been the best teacher any scribe ever had, but what you were teaching would eventually become obsolete, for with books in mass production the world would no longer need scribes. The book-based changes that began with Gutenberg's invention in the 1400s basically went unchanged for centuries. Then the 20th Century – my parents' century – dawned. This was the century for change, significant change, in just one lifetime.

An Era of Rapid Change

Our Information Age technology reinvents itself with startling rapidity. In the 1980s I worked as a training coordinator with an educational television station. My job involved visiting schools and designing workshops to help teachers use instructional television in their classrooms. At that time, I saw the typical equipment in most schools – one or two black and white TVs, sometimes a reel-to-reel videotape recorder, and a TV antenna on the roof. Few schools had access to cable or satellite dishes. If someone had asked me about improving their productivity by using a desktop, laptop, or notebook computer, I would not have known what they were talking about! Furthermore, no one asked about my web site, for such things had not yet been invented.

Now desktop, laptop, notebook computers and web sites are commonplace, and the new technologies I am hearing about change almost daily. Some examples are:

- Wi-Fi connectivity

- Podcasts

- Virtual high schools

- Blogs

- Smartboards

- Bluetooth technology

- Computer adaptive testing

- PDAs, Blackberries

By the time this is in print, I suspect more new technology could be added to my list.

Levels of Technology Implementation

In 1994, Dr. Christopher Moersch developed the Levels of Technology Implementation (LoTi) scale as a way to measure the use of technology in the classroom. The higher levels of his scale focus on using technology as an interactive learning medium, integrated and available in the classroom at all times to support ongoing, purposeful problem solving. The lower levels of his scale target the use of technology to achieve tasks, or do projects such as word processing a report, doing a PowerPoint presentation, developing a slide show, etc. Most classrooms use technology, but most are at the lower levels of his scale. (For more information, log onto www.peak.org.)

To move to the higher levels of technology integration in schools, students need access to technology at all times. To achieve this, some schools issue wireless laptops or PDAs to all students in a given grade level. This a beginning! Using new technologies at the higher levels of the LoTi scale is more interactive. For example, interactive whiteboards allow students to manipulate objects on the screen, not just look at the screen. Students can use the computer to answer multiple choice questions on a test that can then be graded immediately. Teachers who want to differentiate can analyze the test information and group students for instruction.

The Impact of Changing Technologies

What does this mean to us as educators? In one word – **CHANGE**! Rapid change will be the one constant, the defining theme, the way of life throughout the 21st century. Many technological changes have already happened. We have replaced 16 millimeter film projectors first with VCRs and then with DVDs. Overheads are giving way to computer projection units. We have computer labs, laptop schools, and digitized graphic design studies.

Yes, this is change, but the changes that must occur to truly prepare our students for the future must be much more drastic. They must fundamentally change the way we teach. The technology we use in education needs to resemble the technology students are using in other parts of their lives. Technology is not THE solution to education's problems, but it can be a catalyst for positive change to occur.

The meaningful use of technology in schools must go far beyond PowerPoint presentations in the classroom. We need to discover new functions for technology in our schools, not merely ask how technology can help us do the things we already do. If we only continue to do what we have always done, just on a computer rather than in another low-tech way, we'll generally find that technology increases our workload rather than enhancing our productivity. Consider the implications for education:

- Almost all personal computers are as powerful as the super computers of the early 1990s.

- New technologies make it possible to transfer data at lightning speed and to combine text, sound, and video images.

- The merging of a variety of different technologies has the potential to enrich learning experiences.

- Technologies in communications, cable, and entertainment continue to merge.

Students in the 21st century are engaged in technological learning activities such as:
- Exploring geographical locations electronically
- Browsing through the Library of Congress via computer
- Swapping e-mail and instant messages with students in other towns, states, and countries
- Discussing world events as they happen with people all over the world
- Creating multimedia reports that can be accessed by others
- Tracking weather systems, voting patterns, and public opinion
- Creating artistic products via drawing programs
- Hearing a lecture and responding to the lecturer via distance learning
- Working on cooperative projects with students in other locations
- Communicating with a mentor on a specialized topic via computer
- Taking online courses and attending virtual high schools

When considering the possible benefits of technology, it is important to brainstorm all the "impossible" things you would like to do with students. Many of these "impossibilities" can become reality as technology becomes even more powerful and more accessible.

Technology and the Reliability of Sources

21st century students need to develop critical thinking skills along with the ability to understand, evaluate, and integrate information from a wide variety of sources. While technology gives students instant access to unlimited information, students usually pick bits and pieces from the information available and then construct their own set of knowledge, facts, and assumptions in a rather random fashion. This is particularly true when a student 'surfs the Internet.'

Because much inaccurate and misleading information can be found in cyberspace, we must make sure our students are taught to be critical information consumers. Information found on the Internet cannot be understood and correctly analyzed when students merely pick a few sentences, paragraphs, or web sites to look at without evaluating their sources and placing them in context.

When information gathered from the Internet reinforces students' knowledge from past experiences and/or from ideas and facts they have obtained from other media, they can make the connections necessary to analyze and interpret the information. However, when it comes in a vacuum and is not connected to other ideas and experiences, incorrect, unreliable, or biased information is more likely to be taken as truth. This is one of the biggest problems our students face in using technology to do research.

We must take the leadership in showing students how important it is to be critical and evaluative information consumers. This may be the most important skill we teach our students in the Information Age.

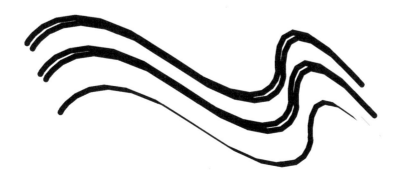

Technology - A 21st Century Teaching Tool

Teacher Reflection Page

1. What are ways I have used technology in my teaching?

2. What successes have I had with technology?

3. What problems have I encountered?

4. What additional uses do I see for technology in my present teaching situation?

5. What could I do with technology in the future that is not possible for me to do now without it?

6. What scares or concerns me about technology?

Educational Applications for Technology

There are limitless ways to use technology to help us educate our students. Six specific ways to enhance educational standards, objectives, and outcomes through technology are discussed below. These applications overlap and are connected to one another. However, it is helpful to look at them as separate entities so we can see more clearly the ways we can use technology to help us carry out our central mission of educating children.

1. Individualize instruction

We've given lip service to individualized instruction in education for a long time. Technology gives us the chance to implement this strategy on a large scale.

With a multitude of technological resources, the curriculum can be much more individualized, fluid, and personalized. No longer does the curriculum need to be driven solely by predigested print materials and texts. Differentiation can happen as teachers prescribe individual learning paths for students who then can move through the lessons at their own pace. Students should no longer be dependent on studying something or doing drill and practice exercises because this is the time in the calendar when all students do this activity. No longer should they be tied to a certain grade level of work when that level is either too hard or too easy.

There are a number of commercially-developed software packages and Internet web site that individualize student learning in nearly every subject. In addition, there are numerous technology packages to help individual students with *NCLB* testing requirements.

Students can create their own individualized curriculum through their own choices of resources. It's important to remember that students need guidance. Without guidance from competent, information-savvy teachers, students may flounder aimlessly for hours looking at snippets of information as they "surf the net" without really accomplishing anything. Even worse, without appropriate teacher guidance and oversight, they may spend their time looking for and at garbage. In fact, one dilemma of the Information Age is that there's so much information it's often hard to find what you want when you want it. That is where the teacher comes in – as the facilitator and guide to students as they become the information retrievers.

This means teachers must be willing to change. Technology-rich classrooms do not have desks in straight rows with the teacher in front. Textbooks and lectures are not the major format for information gathering or new learning. Teachers can truly individualize instruction, but this means the role of the teacher will be quite different.

2. Help students become independent researchers, critical thinkers, and problem solvers

Access to technology greatly enhances students' capacity to do basic research. When students use online tools, databases, and resources, they must also be taught how to analyze and evaluate information. When this happens, teachers should begin to see student research projects that are much more thorough and in-depth. Because students can routinely go online for information, there is no excuse for outdated or incomplete information. Of course, kids will always be kids, so look for new excuses such as, *"The electricity was out so I couldn't do my homework!"*

Productivity tools such as databases, computer graphics, and multimedia authoring programs allow students to organize, analyze, interpret, develop, and evaluate their own work. In other words, using these technological tools can help them learn to be independent problem solvers. Here are examples:

- Picture a math class where students use technology as they collaboratively solve problems, exchange homework, and critique one another's answers. This is a very different scenario from the typical *"Let me copy your math homework"* attitude we sometimes see.

- Consider a class where groups of students use technology to demonstrate problem solving techniques and abstract concepts in many subject areas or in interdisciplinary work.

- Imagine a science class that downloads visual images from satellites and uses up-to-the-minute scientific data accessed online from government agencies. Then picture students developing hypotheses and solving problems based on this information. (One class tracked the paths of all the hurricanes during the volatile 2004 hurricane season using digital satellite images and National Weather Service maps that were available online.)

The three examples above are but a small sampling of how classrooms across America today use technology. The future will hold even more for student researchers and problem solvers.

3. Increase the quality and quantity of student writing and student products

Students often use technology to prepare multimedia projects and presentations. A student doing a research project, for example, can create a report using text, graphics, sound, and video. This is a far cry from the reports of old copied directly from the encyclopedia!

Once multimedia reports are completed, students can present them to their class, or another group of interested people, or store them in a computerized student library, or upload them on a web site for others to use in the future.

Teachers are often concerned about the quality of student writing. Technology, in fact, can help and improve writing. Word processors reduce the phobia some students associate with writing. Technological tools can reduce students' frustration with poor handwriting, grammar, and spelling. With such tools, students can edit and revise written work more quickly and with ease. And the finished product can look great, just as good as something that is ready to be published professionally.

Using a few more technological tools, artistic expression can be nurtured as part of the writing process. Students can enhance their reports using video cameras, animation tools, scanners, digital photography, AutoCAD drawings, and sound. This technology is especially helpful for those students who traditionally have problems in verbal and written communication.

One hundred years ago students came to school with a slate tablet and a piece of chalk. The books, pencils, pens, notebooks, highlighters, calculators, and paper carried by today's students would have seemed an impossible dream in the early 1900s. In the not too distant future, I predict that a notebook computer with wireless Internet access will be part of the school supplies of the average student. In some schools and school districts, this is already the case.

4. Connections with the "real world"

Technology has the potential to allow students to take part in activities and projects that blur the distinction between school and the "real world" as we often call the world outside. When this happens, instead of working on hypothetical problems out of a textbook, students go online and work on the same real-life problems with which other other students, or even adults out there in the "real world," are struggling. They participate in problem solving directly or through simulations, much like the activity done in the workplace.

Helping students share their information and their solutions with others in this way becomes a major step in facilitating their interaction with people outside the four walls of the classroom. Many schools have students involved in creating web sites for their class or their school. Students report that many school alumni visit their web sites to find out what is going on in their Alma Mater.

Telecommunications technology can give students opportunities to work with mentors outside school. Being linked to a mentor in the "real world" via the Internet is a cost effective and exciting way to match students and adults with similar interests.

Technology also can provide a "real world" audience for student work. As our students become linked to the world outside the classroom, their motivation to write and to complete research and other projects soars. After all, real people "out there" are seeing it!

5. Cooperative learning and communication all over the globe

Computers encourage far more collaboration among students in the classroom. As students work together, teachers learn to alter the physical set up of their rooms and modify daily schedules to give students more time to collaborate on projects.

Technology also allows cooperative learning to occur at a distance. Students can team up with students in another school, city, state, or country to work together on a joint project or just to swap e-mail.

Technological tools allow students to inexpensively and instantly reach around the world, learning first hand about other cultures and ideas.

- Teachers and students in London recently had a video conference with teachers and students in Georgia. London students had received Vidalia onions and needed to learn how to cook them!

- A group of high school students in Massachusetts participated in a distance learning session via a satellite hookup with students in Japan. Students on both sides of the globe could see one another on TV and ask each other questions about all kinds of issues.

- Thousands of students all over the United States took an interactive field trip to Kenya . Sponsored by Turner Educational Services and narrated by a reporter, this electronic field trip allowed students to participate in a live, interactive broadcast from Lake Nakunu National Park in Kenya, talk to experts about ecological problems in Africa and in their own communities, and even meet some Kenyan students who showed them how to make sounds like African animals!

Video conferencing and interactive satellite broadcasts such as these that link students not just via the written word, but also through sound and video, are powerful tools for student motivation and learning. Like these groups of students who electronically visited London, Japan, and Kenya, 21st century students will routinely link to all parts of the globe. The results of these interactions will be much more understanding of world problems and of those things that link us all into a "global village."

6. Access to interactive distance learning and online courses

Technology is opening both new ways to learn and a broader range of subject areas to more students. Distance learning via satellite transmission is very different from the old "talking head" seen on instructional television years ago. Instead, it is a new way to deliver information and to give students and teachers access to high-level, high-interest courses and experiences. They can interact with the instructor and with other students, yet remain in a local setting.

For too long, educators based instructional opportunities for students on what the local school could provide. Higher-level courses were often only available in large, wealthy schools or school districts. Interactive distance learning changes all of that. Many more courses are now available to students and also to teachers. Many teachers are receiving advanced degrees earned completely through online course work. AP courses are offered online to students who don't have access to them in their own high school. Some students attend virtual high schools and take some or all of their courses online.

In the electronic learning system of the 21st century, students can listen to a teacher's presentation on television and have access to two-way audio and video systems that allow them to ask questions. We have used television as a teaching tool for decades, but the interactive quality of this approach is its most important feature.

A generation ago one high school student who was taking a televised high school physics course complained, *"I have questions while the teacher is talking. But we're supposed to hold our questions until the once-a -week physics lab. By then, I don't even remember what the question was about! I'm lost if I can't ask my questions as we go along."* In an interactive distance learning system, this student could have asked his questions right away.

Distance learning arrangements between grade levels and schools are becoming much more commonplace. As they do, some of the barriers between grade levels are breaking down. It should not be unusual for a 4th grader, for instance, to take 7th grade math via a distance learning hookup.

Educational Applications for Technology

Teacher Reflection Page

I think most of us agree that new technologies sound wonderful and hold lots of promise for education. As with anything else, there are problems to be overcome. Educational leaders, such as district and school-based administrators, need to consider these problems and concerns. Write your reflections and thoughts about the questions below. Share your answers and your concerns with your colleagues. Finally, it is essential that teachers ask these questions to the administrators and decision makers in the school district.

1. How should teachers be supported through the significant instructional shifts caused by technology?

2. How should teachers be trained so that they are comfortable with and competent in using these new technologies?

3. How are schools going to keep up with ever-changing technologies, both in terms of having the equipment and knowing how to use it?

4. How should we deal with the significant differences in computer literacy, ownership of hardware and software, and access to various technologies between the "haves and the have nots" in schools and school districts, among various classrooms, and within different student populations?

Final Thoughts about Technology

Technology can cause major educational changes. It can facilitate:

❑ Working in teacher teams

❑ Planning and teaching across the disciplines

❑ Modifying school schedules to accommodate ambitious class projects

❑ Integrating several different kinds of media

❑ Instant assessment of student progress while creating appropriate learning activities based on assessment results

Using technology can also significantly change the way you teach. As one high school teacher said:

"As you work with various technologies in the classroom, you start questioning everything you have done in the past and wonder how you can adapt it to the new technologies. Then you start questioning the whole concept of what you did originally. Eventually you learn to undo your old way of thinking."

The array of technological tools for acquiring information, enhancing thinking, and showcasing creativity allows more children more ways to enter the learning environment and succeed. These same things provide the skills that enable students to live productive lives in the global, digital information age of the 21st Century.

Do not underestimate the catalytic impact of technology. It can change the inertia and disinterest so often found in the traditional classroom. It has the potential to:

❑ Encourage fundamentally different forms of interaction among and between students and between students and teachers

❑ Engage students systematically in higher-order thinking

❑ Prompt teachers to question old assumptions about instruction and learning.

As we continue our journey through the technological Information Age, the teacher's role may become more and more "high touch" as many other tasks formerly done by teachers become "high tech." Technology, then, can re-place (that is to say reposition), but not replace, the teacher. Many of those routine tasks now done by teachers can be reassigned to technology, leaving the teacher in a new place educationally to do the things teachers really should be doing anyway. Teachers should be freed to do the work that requires human interaction, continuous assessment, and improving the learning environment. These tasks include:

❑ Building strong, positive relationships with students

❑ Motivating students to love learning

❑ Facilitating the retrieval, understanding, and evaluation of all kinds of information

❑ Identifying and meeting students' emotional needs

❑ Developing student communities and teams for higher-level thinking and problem solving

To see students so engaged in learning that they lose track of time; to see students so excited about learning that they come to school early and stay late; and to see educators who have time to develop strong relationships with their students and who can meet their individual needs ... This is the hope technology gives us.

There are, however, downsides to technology. It requires a steep learning curve for many teachers. Some educators are technophobic or simply do not want to change. The costs of continually updating new technologies can be immense and very difficult in an era of budget restraint.

At best, technology will allow us to fulfill age-old dreams. With it we can individualize instruction. We can enhance student learning through simulations, virtual classrooms, and distance learning. We can take students to new places and introduce them to the "real world." We can give them the tools to create, to write, to do research, and to communicate.

At worst we will use the technology to help us do the same things we've always done. Take this opportunity to go back and reread the other chapters in this book. As you do, reflect upon them in light of the many possibilities technology may hold. Technology could well be the key that will open the door to the many other Teaching Tools for the 21st century.

Reflections

* We live in an era of rapid technological change.

* New technologies have an impact on what happens in the classroom and this impact will grow exponentially throughout the 21st century.

* Technology allows us to teach in many more innovative and exciting ways and allows our students to engage in a variety of new learning activities.

* There are limitless educational applications for technology, but all require teacher planning, imagination, and creativity. They also require teachers to have basic technological skills.

* In an age of "high tech" teachers will be needed more and more for "high touch" work with students that requires human interaction, continuous assessment, counseling, and directing or facilitating learning.

* We need to find a way to deal with significant differences in computer literacy, ownership of hardware and software, and access to various technologies among the "haves" and the "have nots" of the Information Age.

Write Your Own . . .

Student Activities Based on Learning Modalities

Visual

- Draw a

- Write a shape story of

- Design a flag of

- Develop an illustrated brochure of

- Make a collage of

Verbal

- Write a fable about

- Write and recite an ode about

- Write a short play about

- Pretend you are a TV reporter reporting on

- Give a speech about

Student Activities Based on Learning Modalities

<u>Kinesthetic</u>

- Make a T-shirt about

- Write a shape story of

- Construct a scale model of

- Make a classroom museum of

- Make a relief map of

- Create a diorama of

<u>Technological</u>

- On the Internet find out about

- Develop a PowerPoint presentation about

- Use commercially developed software to

- Use a graphics program to

- Develop a multimedia presentation about

Student Activities Based on Learning Styles

Concrete Sequential

- Make an outline of

- Make a calendar for

- Develop a chart showing

- Write a recipe for

- Create a flowchart for

Concrete Random

- Brainstorm possible answers to the question:

- Design a postcard for

- Make a scrapbook of

- Pretend you are a TV reporter reporting on

- Give a speech about

© Carolyn Coil

Student Activities Based on Learning Styles

Abstract Sequential

- Figure out how

- Keep an observation log of

- Write a proposal for

- Give a book review about

- Make an audio tape of

Abstract Random

- With two other classmates, act out

- Explain to your class why

- Interview

- Perform a monologue about

- Organize a panel discussion about

Student Activities Based on Bloom's Taxonomy

Knowledge

- Make a list of
- Identify
- Define
- Label
- Locate

Comprehension

- Design a mural that shows
- Write a paragraph explaining
- List reasons
- Explain why
- Draw a diagram showing

Application

- Make a model of a
- Make a chart showing
- Write an instruction manual for
- Modify or adapt
- Write an editorial about

Student Activities Based on Bloom's Taxonomy

Analysis

- Compare and contrast
- Make a Venn diagram showing
- Predict what might happen
- Dissect
- Analyze

Synthesis

- Develop a plan for
- Write a readers' theater presentation
- Make a time capsule
- Design a new invention to
- Design a proposal to

Evaluation

- Summarize the pros and cons of
- Debate with another student
- Make a "Truth or Fiction" poster of
- Evaluate, according to your criteria,
- Devise criteria to

Student Activities Based on Multiple Intelligences

Verbal/Linguistic

- Write a report explaining

- Tell a legend or fable about

- Write a letter to the editor about

- Write an epic verse about

- Design a word game about

Musical/Rhythmic

- Write a fable about

- Write and recite an ode about

- Write a short play about

- Pretend you are a TV reporter reporting on

- Give a speech about

Logical/Mathematical

- Use a graph to

- Measure

- Figure out the ratio of

- Figure the number of

- Estimate

Visual/Spatial

- Make a set of illustrated flash cards of

- Draw a diagram showing

- Design a set of overhead transparencies for

- Make an illustrated time line of

- Develop a web or concept map of

Student Activities Based on Multiple Intelligences

Bodily/Kinesthetic

- Present a skit of

- Make a model of

- Design a learning center for

- Demonstrate

- Construct

Naturalist

- Describe what kinds of plants and animals

- Research the effect of on the natural environments of

- Make a terrarium of

- Design a shadow for

- Find out about natural methods to

Intrapersonal

- Express your appreciation for

- Write a poem that reflects your feelings about

- Write a letter describing your observations and reflections about

- Write a reflection paper explaining

- Write a journal entry expressing

Interpersonal

- Work in a group to

- Interview

- Design a questionnaire about

- Do a dialog with

- Use pinwheel brainstorming to

Index

A

Ability grouping 175

Abstract Random Learning Style 29, 33, 34, 36, 37, 38, 39, 40, 197, 233

Abstract Sequential Learning Style 29, 31, 34, 36, 37, 38, 40, 233

Acceleration 165, 167, 169, 170, 172-175, 185, 186

Achievement gap 87, 129, 164, 204

Activity chart 26-28

Adequate yearly progress (AYP) 5, 15, 16, 29, 87, 150, 151, 164, 204

Advanced Placement 165,167

Assessment 5, 8, 16-17, 20, 23, 26, 32, 36, 39, 52, 61, 87-115, 116, 118, 120-122, 132, 140, 144, 150-153, 155, 159, 160, 164, 170, 172, 175, 186, 197, 228-229

Authentic assessment 94-95, 112-114, 115, 152, 170

Autonomous Learner Model 165

AYP 29, 87, 150, 151, 164, 204

B

Betts, George 165

Bilingual 128, 129

Bloom's Taxonomy 5, 20, 56-66, 116, 120-122, 159, 169, 197, 234-235

Bodily/Kinesthetic Intelligence 68, 71, 73, 79-81, 83, 84, 86, 118, 120, 159, 237

C

Checklists 16, 81, 91, 94, 96, 98, 115, 176, 209, 211

Choices 12, 14-17, 20, 23, 25, 26, 106, 113, 134, 155, 223

Circle of Respect 208-209

Cluster grouping 166, 175

Coil "4-I" Planning Model™ 6-7

Coil Learning Flowchart™ 116, 117, 122

Compacting 166, 169, 170, 186

Compactor 171

Computer adaptive testing 134, 219

Concrete Random Learning Style 29, 32, 34, 36, 37, 38, 40, 116, 118, 120, 159, 232

Concrete Sequential Learning Style 29, 30, 32, 34, 36, 37, 38, 39, 40, 144, 232

Conflict 5, 76, 102, 127, 141, 147, 176, 188-201

Creativity 8, 30, 88, 111, 116, 118, 119, 120, 122, 155, 163, 164, 187, 228, 229

Criteria cards 8, 94, 96, 104, 106, 115

Cultural characteristics 136, 205, 206

Cultural differences 130

Cultural diversity 5, 127-148

D

Differentiation 16, 23, 39, 56, 59, 91, 115, 122, 152, 153, 160-163, 165-169, 185-187, 219, 223

Disabilities 41, 87, 149-161

Distance learning 168, 175, 220, 225, 226, 229

Dual enrollment 165, 167, 185

E

ELL 129

ENL 129

Enrichment 137, 165-170, 172-176, 185, 186

ESL 128, 129, 133, 134, 138

ESOL 129

Ethnic diversity 127-148

Extensions 39, 106, 119, 165, 167, 172-174, 185

F

Family 135-136, 140, 206, 210, 213, 214

Flexibility 12, 13, 16, 20, 39, 111, 150, 155, 166

Flexible grouping 167, 169, 175

Formative assessment 91-93,114,172